D1073966

VICKERS, George R. The formation of the New Left; the early years. Lexington Books, D. C. Heath, 1975. 166p 74-22460. 14.00. ISBN 0-669-96669-X. C.I.P.

A sociological and historical analysis of the origins of the American New Left. Stress is placed on discussion of two key New Left groups, the Student Peace Union and the Students for a Democratic Society (SDS). Vickers, a sociologist, is mostly concerned with the early period of the New Left, from about 1959 to 1966, and does not deal with the period of greatest strength and impact in the late 1960s. His argument is that the early experiences played a key role in the overall development of the movement and that there were important links with earlier political currents in the American left. One key element of the movement — the civil rights organizations and black power groups — are not treated, as Vickers seems to stress mostly the white, middle-class left. The book is too short to provide a complete analysis, but it is nonetheless a valuable addition to the literature. It complements several other studies, such as Philip Altbach, *Student politics in America* (CHOICE, Apr. 1974), S. M. Lipset, *Rebellion in the university* (1972), and Massimo Teodori, *The New Left: a documentary history* (CHOICE,

Jul.–Aug. 1970). Recommended for scholars concerned with the links between social science and higher education, as well as for students of political activism.

The Formation of the New
Left

The Formation of the New Left

The Early Years

George R. Vickers
Russell Sage Foundation

Lexington Books
D.C. Heath and Company
Lexington, Massachusetts
Toronto   London

Library of Congress Cataloging in Publication Data

Vickers, George.
    The formation of the New Left.

    Bibliography: p.
    Includes index.
    1. Radicalism—United States. 2. College students—United
States—Political activity. 3 Socialism and youth. I. Title.
HN90.R3V52   322.4'2   74-22460
ISBN 0-669-96669-X

Copyright © 1975 by D.C. Heath and Company

Published simultaneously in Canada.

Printed in the United States of America

International Standard Book Number: 0-669-96669-X

Library of Congress Catalog Card Number: 74-22460

To Gil, who bridges the gap.

Contents

Preface		ix
Acknowledgments		xv
Introduction: The New Left as History		1
Theories of the New Left		3
Personal Troubles and Public Issues		9
Dialectics of the New Left		11
Part I	*Seeds of a New Left*	15
Chapter 1	**The End of "The End of Ideology"**	17
	Civil Rights: From the Courtroom to the Streets	19
	A Renewal of Ideology	25
Chapter 2	**Dissent in the Fifties**	31
	The Consolidation of Labor	32
	The Reorganization of the Left	35
	Rumblings in the Silent Generation	45
	The End of an Era	48
Chapter 3	**No Tests East or West**	51
	The Politics of the SPU	52
	The SPU and the Old Left	55
	The SPU: Between Old Left and New	58
Part II	*A Democracy of Individual Participation*	63
Chapter 4	**On Theory**	65
	Out of the Old	66
	Toward a New Left	71
	Port Huron	73
	The Rejection of Liberal Solutions	80
	Toward a New Left Paradigm	86
Chapter 5	**On Practice**	89
	The Formation of an "Elite"	91
	Decision Making and Organizational Structure	94

viii

A Changing of the Guard   98
In Search of Historical Self-Consciousness   101

Part III   Radical Consciousness and Social Process   105

Chapter 6   The New Left and American Society   107

                Education for the Millions   111
                Socialization and the Family   115
                The Changing Class Structure   120
                The New Left in Perspective   121

Chapter 7   Conclusion: The Beginning of the Decline   127

                Resistance and Revolution   128
                The Separation of Culture and Politics   131
                The New Left as a Social Force   132
                The New Left and the Future   136

                Notes   139

                Index   159

                About the Author   167

Preface

In a sense, the final, published version of any social-scientific study has an ahistorical quality. Theories, hypotheses, data, and conclusions are all presented as a kind of *fait accompli,* and the reader may well assume that all that appears in the final product was intended and conceived from the outset. In fact, however, the research process—like the process of history making—is developmental and rooted in a specific context. I hope that by briefly outlining the development of my own research I can alert the reader to be wary of any too rigid separation of research findings from the research process itself.

This study was initially conceived during 1970 and early 1971, in a political climate quite different from that of today. Massive antiwar protests and politically inspired bombings were commonplace, while government countermeasures in the form of grand jury investigations and police surveillance of radicals were mounting. During this period many books and articles appeared offering both scholarly and polemical analyses of the origins and character of the New Left. Of those that reached a mass audience through newspapers or magazines, however, the vast majority were highly critical of the New Left and generally tried to explain it as a tiny minority of psychologically defective individuals.

As one who had been deeply involved in New Left activity since the early sixties—first in the Student Peace Union, then the civil-rights movement, and later SDS and the antiwar movement—I was both intellectually troubled and personally offended by many of these analyses. They did not "ring true" with my own memories of what had occurred. At the same time, I was also troubled by actual developments within the New Left, which I found difficult to comprehend in any systematic way. During conversations with other long-time activists, I discovered that others had similar misgivings, and several of them encouraged me to undertake a major study of the historical development of the New Left from the perspective of one concerned about building and extending the "movement."

I quickly discovered that, despite a voluminous literature on the New Left, very few empirical data were available in secondary sources. I was familiar with James O'Brien's writings on the history of the New Left, but despite the excellent descriptive overview they provided, they contained little analysis of why this history had happened. I was also aware of Richard Flacks's early work on the social bases of activism, and Kenneth Keniston's psychological portrait, but while both of these provided considerable information about the characteristics of individual activists, they did not seem to provide any real insight into what these activists did or why they did it. Given my own background of involvement, my initial intent was to describe the development of the New Left through the eyes of the activists involved, to show how the actions they undertook were a rational response to "reality" as they perceived it, rather than a response to some deep, unconscious psychological urges.

In my initial search for a methodological framework to structure such a study, I remembered E. P. Thompson's *The Making of the English Working Class,* a book that had profoundly influenced me as an undergraduate student in sociology. Thompson seemed to provide exactly what I was after—a description of the formation of a social movement treated as the product of the deliberate activities of the people who made up that movement, while at the same time relating those activities to the larger social networks in which they were enmeshed. As so often with great works of scholarship, however, it is considerably easier to be awed and inspired by Thompson's study than it is to figure out just how he went about doing it. While I was quickly forced to abandon any hope of emulating the comparative framework so central to Thompson's work, the conceptualization of "self activity" as a methodological focus for investigating, and relating, both the objective and the subjective characteristics of social movements began to take shape. This was followed by lengthy explorations of social movement theory and Marxist and neo-Marxist theories, to see how a focus on self activity might add to, or differ from, these theoretical perspectives.

On the basis of these explorations some additional methodological considerations emerged. First, the Marxist notion of *praxis* as the unity of theory and practice—the connection between what people thought and what they did—seemed to offer a useful way of structuring the focus on self activity. Second, the often abstract debate between "orthodox" Marxism and "critical" theory suggested that a serious effort should be made in the analysis of data to examine and evaluate the reciprocal influences of the "substructure" and the "superstructure" on shaping the activity of activists. Finally, the literature on social movements raised issues concerning the relative importance of individual as against organizational characteristics in shaping the development of social movements, and this suggested that the investigation of self activity be clearly placed in the context of organizational development.

In order to address these questions, I determined to seek three kinds of data: data on the actual historical development of the organizations that comprised the New Left, data on the individuals involved in those organizations, and data on structural characteristics of American society that might have influenced those individuals and organizations. As is so often the case in social science research, I next set out to reconcile my view of the ideal data desirable with the constraints imposed by everyday life.

Because of the political climate at the time this study was begun, I first decided to limit the time period of the study in such a way as to exclude any discussion of the development of illegal activities or "underground" organizations. For reasons of convenience, I decided only to examine the development of national organizations of the New Left and their local chapters, thus excluding the vast number of local organizations not directly tied to national structures.

Given these self-imposed limitations, the focus of the study narrowed to a primary emphasis on three organizations: the Student Peace Union, the Student Nonviolent Coordinating Committee, and the Students for a Democratic Society. The national office files of the SPU were available (at the time) at the University of Chicago Library and were supplemented by my own personal files and by personal files of Philip Altbach. The national office files of SDS were available at the State Historical Society of Wisconsin, covering the period from 1962 onward, while the national office files of SDS from 1960 to 1962 were available at the Tamiment Library of New York University. I also obtained access to the personal files of several SNCC leaders.

In addition to these organizational records, I examined files of underground newspapers, published writings by members of the three organizations, publications of the organizations, and personal correspondence made available to me by members of the organizations, in order to develop the organizational histories presented in the text. It became clear, as I compared the development of SDS and the SPU, that the relationship between the Old Left and the New Left was a far more crucial factor in shaping the development of the latter than I had imagined at the outset. In order to explore this relationship, I decided to include an examination of the left in the fifties, and for this purpose used organizational records and documents available at Tamiment Library covering: the League for Industrial Democracy, Student League for Industrial Democracy, Young People's Socialist League, Young Socialist Alliance, Labor Youth League, Socialist Workers party, Independent Socialist League, and Young Socialist League.

To supplement these written records and to gather information on the personal histories of members of the organizations, I also conducted a series of personal interviews. Because the very character of the New Left made it impossible to select random samples of the membership at different points in time, these interviews are biased toward leadership. I interviewed national officers of the SDS between 1962 and 1965, national officers of the SPU between 1959 and 1964, and additional members of those organizations familiar to me through personal knowledge or suggested by other contacts. Where I was unable to locate national officers, I substituted members of the National Executive Committee (SDS) or the National Steering Committee (SPU). I had conducted interviews with a number of SNCC leaders in 1965 and 1966 and did not conduct additional interviews for this study. To supplement the documentation in materials on the Old Left, I interviewed selected persons in different organizations.

The interviews were focused, open-ended interviews and ranged from one to two hours in length. Those interviewed were asked to describe their own family backgrounds; their political views prior to joining the organization; the events and experiences that affected their political views; the internal and external events that, in their view, affected the development of the organization; their perceptions of other individuals in the organization, and their perceptions of other organizations in the Old or New Lefts; and their "analysis" of the origins, nature, and development of the New Left.

In analyzing the data in order to develop the descriptions of organizational development found in the text, the organizational records and the personal interviews were used as cross checks on each other. Where discrepancies existed either concerning the role of particular individuals or concerning the sequence and significance of organizational developments, attempts were made to reconcile these by asking relevant respondents to account for the discrepancies. In all cases, this resulted in eventual agreement or in a vast preponderance of both documentary and interview support for one interpretation. Indeed, the common problems encountered in conducting historical or sociological research with documents were greatly lessened by access to living individuals familiar with the content and context of such documents, while the problems in evaluating individual recollections of past events were lessened by the availability of documents and by access to the recollections of many individuals.

As a result of the analysis of organizational development and personal backgrounds, I was forced to revise my initial assumption that the formation of the New Left could be treated solely as the rational activity of the activists involved. While the diversity of family backgrounds and prior political views reinforced the emphasis on the importance of subjective self activity in shaping organizational developments, certain broad similarities in the educational and occupational backgrounds of activists suggested that the organizational development needed to be examined both in terms of the subjective self activity of activists and in terms of the objective origins of the social base of activists. The sharp clarity with which the self-directed value configurations stood out, moreover, suggested that Flacks was correct in trying to relate the social-class backgrounds with the family socialization process. Melvin Kohn's work, however, suggested a somewhat broader analysis of this process than Flacks had attempted, and Flacks's own findings on the broadening social base of the movement in the late sixties reinforced this suggestion.

As the interpenetration of the objective historical process generating New Left opposition, with the subjective self activity of the activists in creating a theory and practice of the New Left, became more defined, the initial uncritical sympathy with which I viewed the early New Left was transformed into a skepticism about the actual function and objectives of the movement as an anticapitalist political and social force. In this sense, my role of a political partisan and my role as a sociologist created a tension and concern about the implications of this study. At the same time, as the analysis in the text suggests, it seemed to me that any social movement that was unaware of the true sources of its opposition was destined to fail, even in its own terms. Thus, it was precisely because of my partisan sympathies that it was crucial to develop fully the analysis growing out of my work as a sociologist. While I do not claim that such a dual role is free of any difficulties or temptations to distort empirical findings, it may also be better to be clear about one's underlying biases than to assume a kind of neutral "objectivity."

In any case, the completion of this study is only a first step in the larger program of research that will be needed if the events of the 1960s are ever to be fully understood in sociological terms. This study is primarily an ethnographic examination of the major national organizations in the early sixties, and a great many issues about the development of the New Left remain unexplored and unresolved. Whether or not the many local expressions of New Left activity reflect the same characteristics as these national organizations is uncertain. The internal dynamics of the New Left in the late sixties are a matter of speculation here, and the significance of government repression and a broader social base on those developments suggests additional complexities. The dynamics of the black and women's movements, and the relation between these and the development of the New Left in the later period needs to be examined. These and many other issues indicate the continuing need for detailed studies of the New Left. My hope is that by presenting a broad analysis and interpretation of the formation of the New Left, I will stimulate others to reexamine, refine, and extend this analysis to an examination of other issues.

Acknowledgments

It is impossible to list all those who have contributed to the final version of this study, but a few deserve special mention. A Graduate Student Fellowship at the Russell Sage Foundation provided the resources to undertake the extensive research required. Dorothy Swanson and others on the staff of Tamiment Library went out of their way to assist my efforts, and their familiarity with the materials saved much wasted effort on my part. The staff of the State Historical Society of Wisconsin were equally gracious and helpful in providing access to materials not yet ready for public access. Although the Student Peace Union Collection is now at Wisconsin, at the time of my research it was located at the University of Chicago Library.

Kenneth Neubeck offered helpful comments on earlier drafts, and Robert Boguslaw's broad grasp of both quantitative techniques and dialectical theories made him a continuing source of helpful suggestions and penetrating criticism. Tamar Pitch not only read and criticized earlier versions, but her knowledge and grasp of the varieties of Marxist thought provided an invaluable resource. Kristine Aurbakken and Hetty de Sterke struggled with my poor grammar to produce the final manuscript.

Most of all, I owe a profound debt to my many friends and acquaintances in the New Left who agreed to be interviewed and to make available for inspection their personal files and records. Without their encouragement and cooperation the study would not have been possible.

Introduction
The New Left as History

The formation of political consciousness in individuals, and the expression of that consciousness within political movements, is a complex and often mysterious process. To try to understand that process we can survey the political attitudes of individuals and groups, we can compare the political beliefs of children with those of their parents, we can compare one political movement with another and political movements at one point in time with earlier movements, and we can trace the relationship of specific political ideas to broad ideological currents. Once we have described all these patterns, however, it remains extraordinarily difficult to show how these different patterns have combined in a particular way to shape a specific political movement. Even more difficult to discover is *why* these different patterns combined in a particular way at a particular point in time. While improvements in communication, information, and scientific techniques have greatly increased our ability to describe processes of social change, much remains a matter of "artistic guesswork."

This study represents one attempt to explore the networks of social relationships that shaped the character and development of the "New Left" in the early 1960s. Like other such efforts, this study is a mixture of science and informed speculation. I have not examined all, nor even a "representative sample," of the organizations that might legitimately claim to be part of the New Left. Nor were the interviews I conducted based on a representative sample of leaders and members of these organizations. This study is, rather, a kind of analytical narrative describing the formation and development of a few organizations that helped to create that movement we called the New Left. As a part of this narrative, the backgrounds and experiences of some of the participants in these organizations are described, compared, and analyzed.

This study cannot, of course, hope to recapture the feelings shared by those participants in the New Left whose political consciousness and behavior was shaped by the turbulent events of the sixties. Gone are the massive nonviolent protests by blacks demanding "Freedom Now." Gone are the violent conflagrations that tore at the core of America's large cities. Gone, too, are the strident voices calling for revolution in our lifetime —from Sproul Hall at Berkeley, or Fayerweather Hall at Columbia, or, in later years, from "underground." Where once the colorful names and varied initials of New Left organizations vied for the greatest media interest, today the national mass organizations of the New Left are gone —torn apart by a kind of ideological cannibalism.

Most accounts of the New Left have focused on the tremendous expansion of political opposition during the late 1960s and have treated the theory and practice found in the black, antiwar, and student movements of that period as the starting point for an understanding of the character and significance of that New Left. Such a focus may, however, be very misleading. If one begins, not from the massive protests and revolutionary rhetoric of 1968, 1969 and 1970, but from the birth and slow growth of the movement during the early sixties, the events of the later sixties appear in a very different light. If one traces the emergence of a theory and practice uniquely characteristic of the New Left in relation to the theory and practice that characterized the Old Left, the civil-rights movement, and "New Frontier" liberalism during those early years, if we begin with these relationships, we are led to very different lines of inquiry than those typical of other accounts.

Since the New Left was, in its immediate impact, an expression of political protest, it is perhaps not surprising that most analyses of the New Left embody judgments as to its political character and significance. At opposite poles in their political evaluations of the New Left are what we might call "official" and "movement" accounts. The "official" accounts have consistently viewed the New Left as a case of elite manipulation of the nonideological mass of students by a few revolutionaries and have prescribed the isolation of militants as a principal strategy for authorities. Michael Miles has summarized this interpretation:

A hard core of student radicals decides to move against the university. Since they are revolutionary nihilists, these hard-core radicals despise reforms in university polity or structure, but use these issues as pretexts to mobilize student moderates, who are young idealists genuinely concerned about such matters. . . . The objective of the hard core is to destroy the university as a form of sabotage of the American democratic system. They proceed to seize a building or perform some other irresponsible act of force, managing to gain a naive following which is a small minority of the total student population. The point of the initial act of force is to provoke a repression . . . which will immediately mobilize against the authorities a large number of liberals and moderates who were previously uncommitted. Acting according to plan and still in effective control of events, the hard core calls a strike against the university . . . the strike disrupts classes, and sometimes closes down the university for a time, while at the same time radicalizing a large number of students.[1]

The "movement" accounts, while less prone to treat the New Left purely as a *student* phenomenon, present an equally consistent view of its political character. The New Left is viewed as a response by young people and "oppressed" sectors of American society to deep-rooted problems of racism and militarism. These problems are seen as necessary consequences of capitalism, the foreign policies of the United States are seen as manifestations of imperialism, and the New Left is seen as an anti-imperialist, anticapitalist movement of oppressed peoples (including students). The failure of "liberal" administration to eliminate the symptoms and causes of these problems is further evidence of the need for fundamental structural changes, and the New Left must become a revolutionary movement aiming at the eventual seizure of power in order to eliminate these problems.[2]

To go beyond such purely polemical treatments, however, we require an understanding of the sources and character of the New Left, which it is properly the province of the social sciences to provide. And yet, while there is no shortage of written analyses of the New Left, the diversity and mutual exclusivity among supposedly serious accounts is positively staggering. Published analyses differ on the social composition of the New Left, on the psychological motivations of activists, on the structural causes of activism, on the relationship between the Old and New Lefts—indeed, they differ on almost every element necessary for an understanding of the sources and character of the New Left which could provide a basis for evaluating its long-term significance.

Theories of the New Left

Whether they start from psychological, social-psychological, or historical perspectives, social-scientific studies of the New Left share some common problems. The difficulty in achieving scientifically reliable explanations of social movements is nowhere more evident than in the attempts to develop "psychological" explanations of the New Left. These explanations begin from the assumption that certain "personality types" will be attracted to different social movements, and that such movements can be characterized according to the psychological characteristics of their members. Put in extreme form, the psychological approach argues: "The substance of history is psychological—the way human beings have felt, thought, and acted in varying circumstances."[3]

Applied to the New Left, this search for personality types has led to some highly contradictory findings. One author, employing a neo-Freudian comparative history of student movements, found in the New Left "the traits of elitism, suicidalism, populism, filiarchy, and juvenocracy which one found in all student movements, and . . . the interrelation of generational conflict with the special historical circumstances making for the "de-authorization" of the older generation."[4]

Another author, employing a case study of the leadership of one New Left organization, found that the radicals he studied had

developed a sense of inner identity; they have a demonstrated capacity to work, love, and play; they have commitment to their movement; they have a sense of solidarity with others; they feel joined to a radical tradition; and they have more of an ideology than do most adults in America. By such psychological criteria, then, they must be considered adults.[5]

When we turn from psychological studies of the New Left to studies of the "social bases" of New Left activists, we find more agreement. Following the early work of Richard Flacks, a number of surveys of New Left activists have produced a fairly consistent "portrait" of these activists.[6] According to this portrait: activists tended to be recruited from the most selective colleges and universities; seldom had low grades and often seemed to have disproportionately high grades; tended to be more "academic" than nonactivists; tended to be sons and daughters of high-income parents who both had at least four years of college, and who were employed in occupations for which high education is a prerequisite; tended to come from families that are secular and politically liberal; tended to share secular, liberal values with their parents; and tended to come from homes in which a relatively democratic and egalitarian (though not "permissive") child-rearing ideology was emphasized.

Whether they start from the activists' psychological traits and motivations or from their social structural roots, most studies of the New Left attempt a more general theoretical explanation of the emergence of the New Left as a social movement—and at the center of these theories lies the notion of "generational conflict." Starting from the fact that the New Left was comprised of young people, these accounts have sought to explain the New Left in terms either of psychological or of social-structural characteristics of modern youth.

Lewis Feuer, for example, even though his primary focus is on the psychological roots of activism, does treat the New Left as a "student movement" whose characteristics are a special case of the general properties of all student movements. In his view, student movements arise from a dual source: on the one hand, the "conflict of generations" that exists in all societies leads students to see themselves as the bearers of a higher ethic than the surrounding society; on the other hand, this same conflict of generations leads students to a psychological revolt against the established order. This duality of motivations leads to a duality of consequences, and Feuer argues that the traits of "suicidalism" and "terrorism" are invariably present in student movements. This conflict of generations springs from deep, unconscious sources, and Feuer believes that student movements are quite different from other social movements:

We may define a student movement as a combination of students inspired by aims which they try to explicate in a political ideology, and moved by an emotional rebellion in which there is always present a disillusionment with and rejection of the values of the older generation; moreover, the members of a student movement have the conviction that their generation has a special historical mission to fulfill where the older generation, other elites, and other classes have failed.[7]

Feuer argues that student movements tend to arise in societies where the older generation possesses a disproportionate share of economic and political power, as well as social status—what Feuer calls "gerontocratic" societies. The key ingredient in determining whether or not a student movement will arise in such societies is the "de-authorization" of the older generation—the loss of prestige, manliness, etc. among the elders—and this usually results from some sudden or dramatic events. When it does occur, however, youth will be moved by a spirit of "juvenocracy" and a will to "filiarachy" to take advantage of the opportunity and attempt to acquire power. The rapid occurrence of historical crises within a short time span in a given society may lead to more than one "generational conflict" by fostering the simultaneous existence of several political generations, for a "generation" consists of

persons in a common age group who in their formative years have known the same historical experiences, shared the same hopes and disappointments, and experienced a common disillusionment with respect to the elder age groups, toward whom their sense of opposition is defined.[8]

After presenting this psychological model of the sources and motivations of student movements, Feuer then shifts to a discussion of the natural history of student movements, which does not depend on the psychological model for its validity. The first stage in this life history is a "circle stage," which consists of informal groupings of students searching for a standpoint to express their feelings. Once a philosophical perspective has been found, he argues, the movement goes into an "issue-searching stage," which seeks to make concrete the targets of rebellion, and following this the movement enters the stage of "autonomous student action" in which the students begin to develop protest campaigns around the chosen issues. Very rapidly the movement then enters a "back to the people stage," in which populist strains dominate, and depending on the reaction it meets at this stage, the movement then goes through a series of stages until it finally disappears.

Applying this general model of student movements to the development of the New Left in the sixties, Feuer argues that both the black and white student movements of that period began as spontaneous rejections of older generations. The white student movement attached itself to the black student movement, and both of these attached themselves to the broader civil-rights movement (a "carrier movement") in a "back to the people" stage. By 1965, according to Feuer, the New Left had been rejected by the poor it sought to lead, and increasingly turned in upon itself as a vanguard for change. The New Left goal of "participatory democracy" represented, in his view, a kind of democratic anarchy that functioned in a manner similar to Leninism in Russia; its real purpose was to impose a small intellectual elite on the broad masses of people. Although the New Left desired to represent a real social force, in the final analysis, Feuer argues, it was—as all student movements must be—a manifestation of aberrant psychological motivations:

The psychological origin of student movements puts its impress on both their choice of political means and underlying ends. Wherever a set of alternative possible routes toward achieving a given end presents itself, a student movement will usually tend to choose the one which involves a higher measure of violence or humiliation directed against the older generation.[9]

Where Feuer finds in the New Left a conflict of generations rooted in certain Freudian impulses, Richard Flacks sees a rather different process at work:

Emphasis on the youth problem and generational revolt obscures the more fundamental sources of the growing anti-authoritarianism and revolutionary sentiment among white youth in America. . . . What is usually ignored in generational explanations is the social class origins of the most actively disaffected youth.[10]

Based on his own earlier research of the "social bases" of activism, Flacks concludes that the New Left was recruited predominantly from the "educated middle class." Within this broad grouping, certain social-structural and cultural trends converged to create a new class—the "intelligentsia"—whose special characteristic is a combination of high income and education with a family structure and value system that are at odds with traditional capitalist, Protestant culture. He argues that when these characteristics were combined with a particular set of external events in the late fifties and early sixties, the New Left emerged as a social movement. Among the external factors Flacks describes were the concentration of large numbers of this class in universities (allowing a "subculture" of protest to develop), and the catalytic effect of the black student movement (which transformed the personal troubles of young intellectuals into public issues). Although this movement was reformist at the outset, the failure of liberals to respond to the social problems dramatized by the movement quickly led to a growth of revolutionary sentiments. By the late sixties, in his view, the movement had grown numerically and broadened its class base, but had also reached the limits of its potential as a *student* movement.

Although Feuer and Flacks differ sharply over whether the "generational" features of the New Left were rooted in deep psychological traits or in social-structural features of American society, both attempt to explain the ideological and organizational characteristics of the New Left in terms of generational characteristics of the individual participants. James O'Brien also views the New Left as a manifestation of generational conflict, but he is more concerned with its relationship to a tradition of "leftist" dissent in the United States. This leads him to focus on the "public issues" around which protests centered, and in his view, the New Left as a movement was the

creation of young people who graduated from high school and entered college somewhere between, roughly, 1957 and 1966. These young peoples' first picture of politics and society was formed during some part of the interval between the Korean War of 1950-1953 and the decisive escalation of the Indo-China War in the mid-1960s.[11]

O'Brien argues that the critical features of American society during those years that shaped the consciousness of this generation included: the unimpeded growth of corporate capitalism based on military spending; the ideology of militant anticommunism; the decline of militancy in the trade unions; and the suppression and disintegration of the organized left. Two features, in particular, provided the basis for the direction taken by this New Left. One was the accelerating (and increasingly successful) struggle of nonwhite peoples in the "third world" for national liberation from colonial rule. The other was the maturation of the American economy itself, which lost the ability to stimulate a desire to strive for a middle-class life on the part of young people. It was the civil-rights movement, however, led by southern black students, that provided the trigger to release the potentially explosive combination of all these other factors. Following the "sit-in" movement of 1960, issue-oriented protest groups began to spring up on campuses around the country, and it was in these groups that the shape of the New Left began to take form.

This New Left did not spring up everywhere and among all students, however. Based on a content analysis of campus newspapers, O'Brien argues that it grew earliest and fastest at the "elite" colleges and universities, and that it was drawn from among liberal arts students who were not members of fraternities or sororities. He also concludes that it was primarily composed of students who were either children of "old leftists" or children of liberal parents, who were outraged at the conflict between American ideals and practice that the civil-rights movement made manifest. Thus, like Flacks, O'Brien argues that the New Left was an expression of a middle-class intelligentsia, and he agrees that it failed to find a larger base in the population. For him, however, the main significance of the New Left was as a stage in the development of a revolutionary movement:

If we see the New Left in this light, we can avoid the mistakes of judging it by standards that are impossibly high. The New Left, after all, helped to advance immeasurably the conception of how life under capitalism is oppressive and the conception of what revolution might mean in an advanced industrial society. As a result of the experiences and "failures" of the New Left, the American socialist heritage is far richer today than it would otherwise have been.[12]

The studies by Feuer, Flacks, and O'Brien are only three out of the great number of accounts that have been given of the New Left, but their methodological focus and conclusions are typical. These studies vary greatly in their evaluative judgments of the significance of the New Left, as well as in their reliance on psychological, sociological, or historical data to explain the origins and character of that New Left. Despite these differences, however, most academic studies of the New Left share a number of assumptions and conclusions.

Because they start from the *student* character of New Left activists, these accounts invariably search for "causal" factors in age-related features of student life, or in institutional features of the university that generate discontent. In focusing on the phenomenon of "activism," the studies tend to provide a static view of what is a dynamic process. By selecting samples of activist students at particular points in time, these studies can describe the shared individual characteristics of these activists and compare the characteristics of different samples at different times, but they provide little insight into either the personal or structural interactions that produce changes in attitudes, beliefs, or even in social composition. Psychological explanations, in particular, constantly run the risk of isolating the socialization process from concrete social relationships and from historical development. When this occurs, student activism necessarily appears as "deviant," for the "normal" balance of psychological traits appears as a stable reality that existed prior to—and without—activist behavior. Activist behavior thus becomes deviant by definition.

By asserting in advance, for example, that the New Left was a "student movement" whose features were but a derivative of some general sociological property of all student movements, Feuer does not consider the changing social composition of "students," the changing role of universities in American society, or the impact of these changes on the character and significance of a student movement. By rooting the features of student movement in universal "generational conflicts," he avoids the more difficult task of trying to explain the significance of particular student movements in particular societies at particular moments in time.

Flacks and O'Brien pose a related conceptual problem, insofar as their acceptance of the generational features of the New Left restricts their inquiries to an examination of what was different about the *experience* of this generation during their formative years, without at the same time investigating the long-term structural changes that gave rise to those experiences. This results in a useful description of how the New Left was different from earlier generations of students (and of how "activists" were different from nonactivists), but not of why they were different. This latter question is, of course, always the most difficult to answer, but part of the difficulty may lie in the conceptual tools brought to the analysis.

Personal Troubles and Public Issues

C. Wright Mills, in a critical study of the discipline of sociology, argues that the central feature of what he calls the "sociological imagination" is an ability to "grasp history and biography and the relations between the two in society."[13] *Biography,* in Mills' sense, refers to those conditions and circumstances an individual experiences as uniquely his own. *History,* for Mills, refers to those broad changes in social structure that affect the character and direction of whole societies, and within which personal biographies are lived. The importance of this distinction lies in the fact that individuals, in living out their personal biographies, often experience history as a succession of "personal troubles," rather than as "public issues" generated by changing patterns of social structure. Mills argues that it is the challenge and the task of the sociological imagination to distinguish between the personal troubles and public issues that result from individual biographies, and those that result from historical developments over which the individual has little control. Karl Marx posed the same issue in even stronger terms when he argued: "Men make their own history, but they do not make it just as they please; they do not make it under circumstances chosen by themselves, but under circumstances directly encountered, given and transmitted from the past."[14]

With few exceptions (notably Flacks and Keniston), what seems lacking in most academic studies of the New Left is an analysis of the intersection of historical events and personal biography. Put somewhat differently, what seems lacking thus far is an investigation of the actual relationships between "objective conditions" and political "consciousness" in the development of the New Left. You do not *explain* the political behavior or ideology of individuals by describing the common social or psychological backgrounds. Explanation requires that you show the process by which the common social or psychological backgrounds are translated into that particular political behavior or ideology.

There is nothing new about studying the relationships that make up this process. The relationships between the individual and society, between social conditions and ideas, between "experience" and "consciousness" are the special province of the social sciences—particularly of sociology and history. And yet, the record of American sociology in studying these issues leaves much to be desired. The primary focus of sociology in this country has been on the study of "social problems." Since a movement like the New Left constitutes a social problem, insofar as it demonstrates a lack of social "integration," American sociology tends to approach the New Left either as "deviance" or as autonomous "groups and institutions in the process of becoming," which are engaged in a struggle for power with existing groups and institutions. Because the study of social movements has been traditionally defined as part of the study of "collective behavior," this approach has been built into most accounts.[15]

From the standpoint of deviance, the relationship between conditions and consciousness is reduced to a problem of improper socialization or one of individual psychological deficiencies, as in some of the psychological studies of activism. From the "conflict perspective," on the other hand, this relationship is treated as resulting from differentials of power (primarily defined as authority), and "consciousness" becomes equated with "counterculture," as in some of the social-structural studies of activism. These traditions of American sociology have fostered an isolation of the subjective and objective aspects of human behavior into separate spheres of activity, studied independently of one another.

In the study of social movements—particularly in the case of the New Left—this has led to an attempt to explain the ideological and organizational characteristics of the movement in terms of individual traits. The ideological and organizational characteristics of the New Left have been treated either as a direct reflection of the psychological motivations of participants or as an indirect reflection of the social environment, mediated by passive individuals located in that environment. In either of these treatments, however, the individuals who created the New Left are viewed only as objects of history, while the subjective side of their activity is ignored.

If, instead, we look at the New Left as an effort by some individuals living in a particular society at a given time to alter the social environment as they perceived it, then we are led to other perspectives and other emphases. That is to say, the New Left was not simply a kind of stimulus response of individuals to their environment, but it was also a form of self activity by men and women who attached meanings to their actions and experiences. To examine the subjective as well as the objective character of the New Left requires not merely that we examine the beliefs and norms of activists and try to relate these to individual characteristics, but that we investigate the *process* by which conditions, consciousness, and subjective activity become related to one another. In order to do this, however, we must adopt a rather different conceptual framework from those of the studies described earlier.

Dialectics of the New Left

The problem with conceptual approaches that treat the activists of the New Left as largely passive beings, whose behavior is *determined* by psychological or social-structural factors over which they have no control, is that human beings are not merely objects of history; they are also its subjects. Although atypical of the voluminous literature on social movements, some of the concrete studies by social historians remind us that the creation of large-scale social movements by identifiable social groups cannot be fully understood only as *a* response of those groups to structural conditions, but must be seen as *their* response to those conditions.[16] When we look at social movements as the "self-active" creation of identifiable social groups, both the objective conditions that structure that activity and the subjective conditions that impart meaning to it become a focus for investigation.

The guiding framework behind such a focus on "self activity" is what has been called a "relational" view of the world. Within such a framework, the essence of social reality (and thus, the focus for scientific inquiry) consists of the total configuration of relationships among the factors of social life. If an important relationship between some of these factors changes, not only does the total configuration change, but the individual factors comprising that relationship are also altered. This leads to a very different emphasis than the usual social science focus on "causality," as Bertell Ollman has noted:

For the average social scientist—starting with a conception of factors as logically independent of one another—the conjunction of parts in his analysis is mechanical, an intrusion. . . . One result is the endless attempt to account for causality and the accompanying need to distinguish between cause and condition. In such studies, one side of the interaction invariably wins out over the other ("comes first") leading to "economic determinism" or "existentialism" or other partial positions.[17]

From a relational framework, however, the conjunction of parts is organic, is intrinsic to the social units with which we are concerned and part of the nature of each. As Ollman also notes, to focus on the "inner connections" of social factors is to go beyond the mere recognition that social factors are related to one another:

The outlook presented here must not be confused with the view that has found great favor among sociologists and others, which holds that social factors are *unintelligible* except in terms of relations. It is important to realize . . . the additional steps indicated in his claim that society is "man himself in his social relations."[18]

In the relational view of the world, change and development are constantly occurring. The present becomes part of a continuum that stretches from a definable past to a knowable (if not predictable) future. Thus, the character of the New Left as a *left* can only be understood in relation to the left that preceded it. Moreover, to understand the relationship between the subjective and the objective processes that shaped the development of the New Left, we must begin not with a search for strict causal ties between the mode of production and other institutions, but with an acceptance that complex interaction occurs and a search for the ways in which the mode of production affects that interaction. Throughout this account, then, I have avoided trying to identify some factors as *causing* specific characteristics of the New Left and other factors as being *conditions* for that development. Instead, I have attempted to show how the various factors shaped the total set of relations that characterize the New Left, and to indicate in specific context which relations seem the most helpful in understanding the relevant characteristics.

This relational view of the world is most easily expressed in the language of the "dialectic," and throughout the study I have organized my presentation around key elements of the dialectical outlook. In the discussion of both the subjective and objective processes, I have focused on the transformation of *quantitative* changes (whether in terms of the number of activists or in terms of changes in the occupational structure) into *qualitative* changes (e.g., the nature of the left, or the character of the class structure); the mutual penetration of polar opposites—that is, the way in which factors that appear to be diametrically opposed are linked to each other in order for their own existence to have meaning (e.g., the theory and practice of the Old and New Left); the notion of development through contradiction (e.g., the way in which the objective character of the New Left as a rationalizing force also made it an oppositional force); and on the spiral form of development (as when the splintering of the New Left seems to copy the pattern of the Old Left in the fifties—but with a difference).

Put in such abstract terms, however, the perspective I have employed is primarily a tool for theoretical and methodological debate with other perspectives. The real issue is, and should be, the extent to which this perspective helps us to understand the sources and character of the New Left. My primary purpose is not to reexamine earlier studies of New Left activists or to reexamine previous descriptions of the historical development of the New Left, but to use these earlier studies as a starting point for an investigation that treats the development of the New Left as part of the historical development of American society. The account is *historical* both because what is "new" about the New Left can be understood only in relation to what preceded it, and because any study of social change must look at developments over time. The account is *concrete,* because it is primarily an empirical investigation of the development and character of specific organizations, rather than an exercise in the history of ideas. While I have borrowed heavily from empirical studies of the structural and psychological roots of New Left activism, the major discussion of organizational and ideological development is based on a series of interviews with members of those organizations and on organizational files and personal correspondence.

The study is divided into three parts. The first part focuses on the connections between the New Left and earlier traditions of political dissent and seeks to locate some of the features of a New Left in the broader political climate of the late 1950s and early 1960s. In the second part, the focus shifts to an investigation of the gradual development of a theory and practice of the New Left as a response to the backgrounds and experiences of the activists themselves. From this exploration of the "self-active formation" of the New Left in the first two parts, the final section returns to an examination of the connections between the formation of a New Left and long-term changes in the social structure of American society.

In exploring the development of a New Left theory and practice, this account focuses on the development of two national organizations—the Student Peace Union and the Students for a Democratic Society—not because all facets of the New Left can be understood through an examination of these organizations, but because they involved the largest number of participants and because a comparison of their developments highlights some of the key differences between the Old and the New Left. At the same time, however, such a narrow focus can only begin to sketch the outlines of the social processes involved. The New Left was nothing if not varied, and the specific experiences of participants in a variety of locales, each with its own unique features and problems, profoundly affected the patterns of development. A full understanding of the process of formation of the New Left will require many more detailed examinations of that process in specific settings, as well as a systematic examination of the New Left in the late sixties. Thus, this is not the "definitive" study of the nature of the New Left, but it is my hope that I have succeeded in identifying some of the major issues that such a study must address.

PART I

Seeds of a New Left

I see the rise of a New Left in this country, a Left of a nature that has not been seen within this century. It will be a Left unconnected with the past. . . .

Instead a New Left is coming, a Left of "independent radical activity": non-partisan, indiscriminate in its condemnation of reactionaries and old-style radicals, not inclined to organization (which will make it difficult to trace its rise), and uncapturable by either the splintered old Left or by progressive elements in present major parties. . . .

But I know—and I am not alone in my feeling—that this decade will make a great deal of history. . . . Rather than delay its birth, the events since the war have been most necessary and have gone a long way toward shaping what will come. So much silence will have an out, and a peculiar and potent one indeed.

(Letter from Michael Rossman,
May 20, 1960, Reprinted in
The Wedding Within the War,
Garden City, N.Y.: Doubleday, 1965)

1

The End of "The End of Ideology"

From June 11 to 15, 1962, fifty-nine young people gathered at the United Auto Workers conference center, in Port Huron, Michigan, to discuss the prospects for a new student left in the United States. Ostensibly a national convention of the Students for a Democratic Society (SDS), the Port Huron meeting brought together a wide range of student "activists" to develop a "statement of conviction and program for the young left in America." The only condition for membership in the SDS was a commitment to democracy "as a means and as a social goal,"[1] and what was meant by democracy was spelled out in the *Port Huron Statement:*

As a *social system* we seek the establishment of a democracy of individual participation, governed by two central aims: that the individual share in those social decisions determining the quality and direction of his life; that society be organized to encourage independence in men and provide the media for their common participation.[2]

On July 23, 1970, a grand jury in Detroit, Michigan indicted thirteen leaders of the SDS on charges of "conspiring to bomb and kill," and that same year a committee of the United States Congress declared:

From a study of SDS, we can acquire new insight into how such [revolutionary] movements may be generated, motivated, enlarged, and ignited into serious threats to our society, our Government, educational institutions, national security, and international obligations and responsibilities.[3]

In order to achieve its objective of a "democracy of individual participation," the first generation of SDS leaders had called for the creation of a "New Left" that

must transform modern complexity into issues that can be understood and felt close-up by every human being. It must give form to the feelings of helplessness and indifference, so that people may see the political, social and economic sources of their private troubles and organize to change society.[4]

The generation of SDS leaders indicted in 1970 declared as its objective "the destruction of US imperialism and the achievement of a classless world: world communism,"[5] and called for the creation of a "revolutionary youth movement" to accomplish this objective. By 1971 the SDS no longer existed, its indicted leaders having gone "underground" to direct a cam-

17

paign of bombing and guerilla activities. The "New Left" that SDS had sought to create seemed, instead, to have copied the pattern of the Old Left by splintering into a number of hostile, warring sects isolated from the mainstream of American society.

Of all the organizations that came to be associated with the New Left, the Students for a Democratic Society was by far the largest and best known. Between 1965 and 1970, almost all of the activities associated with the New Left took place within the SDS framework. The SDS appeared suddenly on the political scene after its Port Huron convention in 1962, and both to outside observers and to its members, it seemed to represent something "new," a break with the political and organizational hegemony over dissent that had been exercised by an older left that had grown in the thirties and dwindled in the years following World War II. Although it was concerned with many of the same issues as that earlier left, in its "style" and composition the SDS marked a break with the traditional characteristics of the American left.

No important change in the locus or character of political activity develops entirely free of the past, however. Whatever else it may be, political activity is *organized* activity—it involves people who share common goals working with each other to achieve those goals. And whatever differences or similarities there are in the backgrounds and motivations of persons involved in political activity, these differences or similarities have their most immediate impact on the structure and programs of the organizations which individuals create to further their objectives. Political organizations become crucial reference points for those involved in political activity—the place where the significance of events is interpreted, where analysis of events is developed, and where the common bonds of membership take on form and substance.

Precisely because political activity *begins* as organized activity, any investigation of major shifts in the character of political activity must begin with an investigation of the origins, structure, program, and composition of the political organizations that initiate such shifts. Sometimes these are the result of "splits" within older organizations, and sometimes they are "new" organizations without formal ties to the past, but always they emerge from a process of change that begins within the prior framework of organized political activity. The development of a New Left was no exception to this process, and despite many differences from an older left, the organizational beginnings of the New Left emerged within, and out of, the political framework of the fifties. The actual name came from Britain, where a group of former communists and "old leftists"—disillusioned by Hungary and the revelations about Stalin—began a new journal at the end of the fifties, *The New Left Review*. If we choose the issuance of the *Port Huron Statement* as a public birthdate of the New Left in America, then the seeds of that New Left can be found years earlier in the changing character of political activity among blacks and students.

Civil Rights: From the Courtroom to the Streets

The history of black people on this continent has been a history of struggle by many means, including slave revolts, nationalistic movements, legal battles, electoral protest, and direct action of both a violent and nonviolent character. Just as there have been attempts by blacks to adapt to, and assimilate with, the dominant white culture, there have also been repeated protests against the unequal treatment of blacks by white society. Often different forms of protest have gone on simultaneously, as during the early part of this century when Marcus Garvey's "Back to Africa" campaign gained popularity at the same time that "race riots" with distinctly political overtones were occurring.[6]

With the coming of the New Deal, northern blacks gained a limited amount of influence within the Democratic party, and protest shifted to the ballot box and to legal challenges based on the Fourteenth Amendment. These efforts led, in the forties, to an executive order prohibiting discrimination in employment, and to a Supreme Court decision declaring the "restrictive covenant" in housing contracts unconstitutional. In the South, however, legal segregation of the races remained the central feature of the southern "way of life," and southern blacks continued to face the daily humiliations of segregation: separate but unequal facilities, racial slurs, and inferior jobs and pay.

The legal strategy finally resulted, in 1954, in a Supreme Court decision that declared segregated schools "inherently unequal" and ordered that schools in the South be integrated with "all deliberate speed." At last, it seemed that the modest gains won earlier in the North would spread to the South, and that the uneven development of race relations in different regions of the country would begin to equalize.

Throughout the country, the main black organizations that coordinated and initiated efforts to improve the legal and material conditions of blacks were the National Association for the Advancement of Colored People and the National Urban League, both of which drew their membership from the black "middle-class" of clergy and professionals. The dominant ideology behind these efforts was assimilationist in thrust, with "integration" of blacks into previously all white institutions as the major objective. Although there have been notable exceptions to this pattern, such as the Niagara movement and other forms of "nationalist" ideology,[7] by the late nineteen-fifties, the integrationist theme was clearly dominant. The nationalist theme was reasserted during the sixties by the Black Muslims and Malcolm X, and by the end of the decade the situation was reversed from the fifties.

In 1955, a different kind of protest took place, which, although it was not to be repeated until the early sixties, signaled the beginning of a change in both the social composition and the organizational form of black protest. The Montgomery bus boycott involved almost an entire community of 50,000 blacks in a sustained and collective confrontation with a local white "power structure" for more than a year.

The eventual success of the boycott was due to several ingredients: setting a "reasonable" integrationist goal that was difficult to discredit; developing a cadre of leaders who could work together and who were representative of the community; developing an infrastructure that could mobilize and maintain a boycott for thirteen months; creating support from the outside that provided publicity and finances; and obtaining judicial intervention to force an eventual settlement. These same ingredients would be further tested and developed in the civil-rights campaigns of the sixties, but at the time they were novel and not quickly adopted by groups like the NAACP. To foster the application of the "direct action" techniques developed in Montgomery, King formed the Southern Christian Leadership Conference, whose primary base was among the black clergy in the South.

During the remainder of the fifties, the civil-rights strategy focused on the South and aimed at first desegregating, then integrating, all-white institutions. The NAACP concentrated on a state-by-state, county-by-county legal campaign to force compliance with the 1954 Supreme Court decision on school desegregation. The SCLC directed its efforts at "exporting" the direct action techniques of the Montgomery campaign to other cities, and the Congress of Racial Equality divided its activities between organizing parents for the confrontations that often took place on the first day of school and initiating direct action protests at segregated public facilities in a few border states.

Even at the time of the Montgomery campaign there were signs that something more than simple protest might be needed before segregation could be ended, and that a whole system of domination would have to be challenged and overcome by concerted political struggle. As Martin Luther King put it after the Montgomery experience:

Feeling that our demands were moderate, I had assumed that they would be granted with little question; I had believed that the privileged would give up their privileges on request. This experience, however, taught me a lesson. I came to see that no one gives up his privileges without strong resistance. I saw further that the underlying purpose of segregation was to oppress and exploit the segregated, not simply to keep them apart. Even when we asked for justice within the segregation laws, the "powers that be" were not willing to grant it. Justice and equality, I saw, would never come while segregation remained, because the basic purpose of segregation was to perpetuate injustice and inequality.[8]

From Direct Action to Political Organizing

The year 1960 marked the beginning of a profound change in the character and composition of civil-rights activity. On February 1 of that year, four freshmen at A & T College in Greensboro, North Carolina sat down at a segregated lunch counter in the local Woolworth's and refused to leave after being denied service. They were arrested and jailed, but their action triggered a series of demonstrations that, within a few short months, transformed the organizational character of civil-rights protest from that of a collection of small organizations seeking to erode century-old patterns of discrimination, into a massive social movement demanding "Freedom Now!" During the first month of the "sit-in" campaign that spread from Greensboro, black students from no fewer than twenty-six different colleges and universities participated in direct action, and the following month students from twenty-seven more institutions joined the protest. Within the next year, more than 50,000 persons had participated in some kind of demonstration in more than one hundred cities, and over 3600 demonstrators had spent time in jail.[9]

The student sit-in campaign was spontaneous in the sense that none of the existing civil-rights organizations had planned and directed the campaign, but it was not unorganized. For example, the first sit-ins of the campaign in Tallahassee, Florida took place on February 13, but they were led by a CORE group formed the previous October.[10] In Nashville, plans to launch a campaign to desegregate restaurants had been underway since the fall of 1959, and training sessions in nonviolent direct action had begun that same fall, although the first sit-ins of the campaign were not held until February 13. In cities where existing civil-rights groups did not lead the initial sit-ins, organizers from CORE or SCLC were quickly sent in to assist with the actions.

What the sit-in campaign did was to bring together in the context of direct action a new combination of forces. While all of the adult groups were primarily composed of "middle-class" blacks, their political composition was more distinctive. The NAACP included many leaders of organized labor, as well as some blacks and whites with ties to the "social-democratic" left (e.g., the League for Industrial Democracy). Groups like CORE had strong ties to the pacifist left and the Socialist party, while SCLC was tied to pacifist clergy. The student sit-in campaign brought all these diverse political elements under one framework, as well as elements of the Communist left of the fifties, although it retained the "middle-class" character of the adult groups.[11] The problem for such a diverse grouping was to find an "ideology" that could hold these elements together in the context of action, and that ideology emerged in the form of a particular conception of *nonviolence* developed during the campaign.

The leaders of the civil-rights organizations were confronted with problems of both a psychological and political character in transforming isolated protests into a mass movement. The psychological problems were similar to those that Frantz Fanon found among natives in colonized Africa.[12] Many blacks had been kept in inferior positions for so long that they had come to accept that inferiority as "natural." Often, their anger against whites was sublimated and projected against other blacks, and hopelessness was widespread. In order to overcome these psychological obstacles to political activity, the civil-rights leaders developed symbolic demonstrations which showed black people struggling against their oppression. At the same time, they had to produce at least some victories to communicate the hope that collective action could bring a change. But to win such victories, the black movement needed powerful allies in the white community, since blacks had little institutionalized economic or political power. By focusing on the South, the civil-rights leaders were able to exploit the disparities in race relations between North and South, and could appeal to northern liberals for economic and political support. In order for this appeal to succeed, however, they had to discourage fears that their actions threatened liberal interests or the "fabric of social order"—that is, they had to place the burden for any social disruption that occurred on their southern white opposition.

Nonviolence provided the mechanism for accomplishing these tasks. By rigidly avoiding physical violence it allayed fears that the protesters sought violent confrontation; by appealing to the moral conscience of "men of good will" it obscured class divisions and encouraged wide support; and through its use as a *mass,* rather than individual, technique of direct action it aided in building a sense of the potential of collective action and encouraged a kind of moral superiority among its users. It was, in the words of one of the classic writings on nonviolence, a form of "moral jiu-jitsu." The technique itself was not new, of course, but the American civil-rights movement provided a major test of its potential as a means of struggle by a minority group, rather than by a whole population, as in India.

Not all of these considerations were carefully thought out at the time, of course, but the main lines were debated and discussed. In Nashville, a group of students from various black colleges began meeting with the Reverend James Lawson (a member of the Fellowship of Reconciliation and a World War II draft resister) in the fall of 1959.[13] At the time, Lawson was perhaps the chief theoretician of nonviolence in the country, as well as a socialist, and over the next year the Nashville group built a powerful mass movement that achieved the first victories against segregated lunch counters and went on to win other concessions from the city. Out of this Nashville group came future leaders of the SCLC such as James Bevel, C. T. Vivian, and Kelly Miller Smith, and future leaders of the Student Nonviolent Coordinating Committee such as Diane Nash, Bernard

Lafayette, John Lewis, Marion Barry, and Lester McKinnie. From the earliest days of the study group, the Nashville people coupled the tactic of nonviolence—and for many of them it was a personal philosophy as well as a tactic—with social objectives that went far beyond "desegregation" and "integration" toward a conception of the need to fundamentally restructure American society. The influence of this group had its most direct impact on the Student Nonviolent Coordinating Committee, and through SNCC on the white New Left.

In late February of 1960, leaders of the SCLC felt that local sit-in leaders should be brought together to discuss and coordinate their efforts, and a conference was called for Easter weekend in Raleigh. Over two hundred students attended the conference, and by May of that year the Temporary Student Nonviolent Coordinating Committee was formed. Many of the students involved in the formation of SNCC were of "middle-class" origins, and their Statement of Purpose confirmed the adoption of nonviolent mass action as the central tactic of student efforts: "We affirm the philosophical or religious ideal of nonviolence as the foundation of our purpose, the presupposition of our belief, and the manner of our action."[14]

Although there was a great deal of pressure at the conference for the students to become a youth wing of either SCLC or CORE, the students decided to remain autonomous. During the remainder of 1960, SNCC continued to organize local sit-in campaigns, and many of its "field workers" participated in the CORE-initiated Freedom Rides the following year. SNCC was not a membership organization, however, but was a "committee of organizers." Persons who were considered part of SNCC did not concentrate on recruiting members, but on planning and carrying out a strategy for building a South-wide mass movement of blacks. While other civil-rights organizations were still thinking in terms of desegregation and integration as their main objectives, SNCC was already laying plans for a long-range effort to build a political base among southern blacks.

At a SNCC conference in the fall of 1960, for example, while the sit-ins were still the main activity and before the Freedom Rides had begun, keynote speaker James Lawson called for a "nonviolent revolution" to revamp the entire society.[15] Discussion of the desirability and possibility of making a "revolution" spread rapidly in SNCC circles, and by the fall of 1961 a future leader of the SDS travelling in the South could observe:

Most important is the crazy new sentiment that this is not a movement but a revolution, that our identity should not be with our Negro predecessors but with the new nations around the world, and that beyond lunch counter desegregation there are much more serious evils which must be ripped out by any means: exploitation, socially destructive capital, evil politics and legal structure, and myopic liberalism which is anti-revolutionary. *Revolution* permeates discussion like never before. . . . In our future dealings we should be aware that they have changed down here, and we should speak their revolutionary language without mocking it, for it is not lip service, nor is it the ego fulfillment of a rising Negro class, but it is in truth the fact of life in the South this minute.[16]

Debates about the proper organizing strategy were vigorous throughout 1961, with many in the organization urging a continued emphasis on demonstrations and civil disobedience, while others favored shifting to a voter registration campaign. The latter course had been proposed by Tim Jenkins, a black vice-president of the National Student Association, and there were indications that the Kennedy administration and certain foundations were urging this course—all of which made many SNCC activists fearful of being "co-opted." Finally, however, a decision was made to go ahead on both fronts: Diane Nash was put in charge of the direct action campaigns, and Charles Jones headed up the voter drive. Bob Moses was already in Mississippi setting up voter registration schools when the decision was made, and he was added to the staff to handle Mississippi.

As the voter registration drive took SNCC into local communities across the South, the composition of the staff began to change, and what had been a predominantly "middle-class" organization of students during the sit-ins, now became a disciplined group of nonstudents and ex students, mostly from poor backgrounds.[17] The voter registration drive increasingly became the dominant approach of SNCC, and those in the organization favoring direct action began to gravitate toward SCLC. By 1963 this difference between strategies also began to manifest itself in political and organizational differences between the two organizations.

The move away from the campuses and into local communities also produced a different organizing strategy than that which had characterized the civil-rights movement up to that point. So long as the objectives of the movement were desegregation and integration, the technique of mass nonviolent direct action could be applied in concentrated doses to symbolic targets. A specific target (such as segregated buses) could be selected, a cadre of leaders could then move into a given community to build a mass movement focused on that target, and after victory or defeat the leaders could move on to other targets in other cities. The psychological obstacles were overcome in the process of mobilization, and the need for concrete victories was satisfied through legislative or judicial intervention. This was the program that had been developed in Montgomery, failed in Albany (Georgia), and succeeded again in Birmingham and Selma. In a certain sense, this strategy treated local communities as instrumental to a broader struggle, and because its objectives in any given community were limited and specific, no long-term organization of the local population took place.

Building a base of black political power throughout the South, however, required that permanent organizations be built in local communities. The task of the "committee of organizers" was to go into a community, develop local leadership and organization, and then move on to repeat the process in other communities. This was no small task—as the SNCC organizers quickly learned. As soon as a SNCC worker arrived in a rural Mississippi town, he attracted the attention and hostility of the local white power structure, and when he moved on it was the local blacks who had to face the backlash of that hostility. Furthermore, local conditions often varied from community to community, and from state to state, and the organizers had to be sensitive to these differences.

This led to a form of what might be called "catalytic organizing," where SNCC workers acted as a stimulus, resource, and example to the local population, but shunned formal leadership. Just as the sit-ins and freedom rides had been "exemplary" actions, insofar as they served as models of individual and collective struggle against oppression, so the SNCC field workers sought to provide an example of free blacks exercising their rights. Another consequence of this approach, however, was that the SNCC workers avoided giving strong political direction to the local blacks, insisting, instead, that the local community define its own needs and objectives, which the SNCC worker would then help them to achieve. In the historical context of the political development of southern blacks, this approach represented a necessary stage in building the psychological and organizational base for a political movement, but its later adoption by the white New Left led to consequences that could not be foreseen in the fall of 1961.

Thus, by the end of 1962, the form, composition, and objectives of the civil-rights movement had begun a profound transformation. From a largely middle-class beginning as an attempt to broaden the areas of racial equality in American life, the movement had begun to broaden its base in the black community and to face the imperatives of a political struggle for social and economic power. This transformation had only begun in 1962—Birmingham, the March on Washington, and Selma all lay in the future—yet, the seeds of this new struggle had been planted in Mississippi. While the older organizations continued to play an important role in the civil-rights campaigns in the early sixties, it was the activities of the young SNCC workers which shaped the political direction of that struggle. It was also their activities which crystallized and gave form to the feelings of discontent among a new generation of white college students. This discontent had begun to find organized expression in the last years of the fifties, but the SNCC actions served to bring diverse groupings together in support of the southern students. In the process of this coming together, the search for collective definitions of their discontent began to develop.

A Renewal of Ideology

If the decade from 1945 to 1955 witnessed the "end of ideology," marked by the decline and disintegration of an American left,[18] then the waning years of the nineteen-fifties witnessed a renewal of critical political thought which laid the foundation for a New Left to emerge in the early sixties. This new interest in politics began to develop as early as 1958, and it was first noticed by younger members of the Old Left, who found it difficult to comprehend. At the outset, this new interest included a fundamental questioning of the meaning of political activity, and this questioning reflected the extent to which old strategies of protest seemed bankrupt. Some of the elements of this new interest, as well as the surprise it caused among those who were radicals during the "silent generation," are reflected in a letter from one member of the Wisconsin Liberal Club in 1959:

It is also interesting to note that the *very same* topics we tossed about last summer, which failed to raise much enthusiasm, now have been proposed almost spontaneously by these people: all of whom I had never met before. . . .

While we are not in accord on all points, it is to me remarkable that at our first meeting this afternoon, we did all seem to feel that: a) there is a need for redefinition of the term "Liberal" and that it must include a scope of human thought and action of which political and economic views are only a part; b) the basis of such a "Liberal" outlook is a free, unfettered, critical inquiring mind; c) that no existing political/economic dogma is a sole means to an end; d) that problems facing society today cannot be answered solely in terms of existing social/political/economic theories. In short, the group is a collection of dissatisfied intellectuals, who for reasons of internal consistency cannot adhere to the traditional political dogmas.[19]

For the most part, however, this new interest in politics did not lead to a numerical growth of older left organizations, but, instead, to the formation of "independent" political organizations not tied to existing groups.[20] One reason for this was that, despite the new interest, students were wary of being identified with specific ideologies they neither fully understood nor saw as offering any promise of change. Another letter from the Wisconsin Liberal Club elaborated these fears:

One last topic of discussion before I close—the possibility of WLC breaking its affilitation with SLID. . . . One reason for the possible severance is the feeling by some of the members that, though they are liberals, they ain't that liberal! SLID's past is too closely associated with Socialism for most of our members to forget or overlook the connection. And I am sure that many of our members, myself included, are not even close to being Socialists, at least not 1930s' Socialists.[21]

Instead, the new interest in politics developed in two directions: toward the creation of "multi-issue" organizations that sought to connect and explain a series of issues with the aim of eliminating their common root causes; and toward the creation of "single-issue" organizations seeking to mobilize protest around one issue. The multi-issue approach first took the form of campus political parties on campuses with a history of political activity. As was the case through much of the sixties, the University of California at Berkeley set the example for such activity when, in early 1958, a coalition of students from religious groups, co-ops, "independents," and Old Left radicals formed SLATE (Slate of Candidates) to compete with fraternities for control of the student government.[22] In an early statement, SLATE outlined its broad aims:

We will be concerned with students as citizens in society—with their involvement with national and international issues.
We will be concerned with education—with whether or not the University helps us to be open-minded, thinking individuals.
We will be concerned with academic freedom and civil liberties.
We ask only a fair hearing in the open market-place of ideas.[23]

Within three years, similar student parties were formed on a number of large campuses, including POLIT at the University of Chicago, SCOPE at the University of Illinois, DECLARE at the Riverside Campus of the University of California, and VOICE at the University of Michigan.[24] All of these were multi-issue, unaffiliated student parties initiated by radicals, but included many students new to political activity. Beginning in the summer of 1959, SLATE sponsored annual conferences that brought these parties together with other student political groups like the Young Democrats, Young People's Socialist League, CORE, NAACP, etc., to discuss common positions on issues like civil liberties, civil rights, and disarmament. As the idea of student political parties began to spread, a new national network of communication of political ideas developed, and as these parties altered the character of student government on large campuses, existing forums like the National Student Association Congress became arenas for organizing and recruiting around left proposals. Despite the spread of these multi-issues organizations, however, they remained primarily *local* centers without formal national structure, maintaining loose and informal communications with similar groups.

It was the "single-issue" organizations which first developed coherent national structures, and the largest of these were the groups protesting the nuclear arms race. The cold war between the Soviet Union and the United States had led to massive stockpiling and testing of nuclear weapons by both sides, and as the nuclear age entered its second decade, debates about strontium 90 in milk and Roentgen levels in radioactive fallout joined with policy debates about "deterrence" versus "counterforce" strategies of national defense to produce a broad national debate on defense, foreign policy, and survival in the nuclear age.[25]

In 1957, a group of nonpacifist liberals took out an ad in the *New York Times* criticizing the reliance on nuclear weapons and warning of the danger of accidental war. Although intended as an ad hoc committee whose sole purpose was to sponsor and finance this ad, the outpouring of favorable response from around the country forced the National Committee for a SANE Nuclear Policy to continue as a coordinating committee to initiate educational and lobbying efforts concerned with disarmament.[26] Although SANE never became a "mass" organization, it did mark the first significant return to political activity by left-liberals since the beginning of the cold war. By 1960, additional adult groups were forming, and attempts to link up liberal and pacifist approaches were under way. In all these attempts, however, Old Left parties were prohibited from participating as organizations, and anti-Communist rhetoric was routinely included in the statements and literature of such groups.

In 1958, a Student Committee for a SANE Nuclear Policy formed independently of the adult organization, but was quickly accorded recognition as a student affiliate. Unlike the adult group, however, Student SANE was dominated by youth close to the Communist party.[27] The student group spread to a number of campuses over the next few years, but when Senator Thomas Dodd threatened a public hearing into Communist infiltration of adult SANE, the adult organization amended its constitution to exclude Communists from membership. The student group refused to follow this policy, and after a series of conflicts the student group was suspended in 1962, after which it declined rapidly.

While liberal opposition to nuclear testing centered around SANE, the older pacifist organizations centered their activities in direct action campaigns at military bases and at testing sites. In December of 1960, the Committee for Nonviolent Action initiated a major educational protest in the form of a San Francisco to Moscow Walk for Peace and, in the course of this walk, passed through literally hundreds of towns and cities handing out literature and making visible their protest. In a number of these cities, annual Easter "peace walks" were continued for several years by local residents, as protest activities spread out from traditional centers such as New York and San Francisco.

The "single-issue" and "multi-issue" organizations that sprang up in the last years of the fifties represented not only a *revival* of critical politics, but also a *transition* between an Old Left that had matured in the thirties and a New Left yet to be born. Within these organizations, the crucial differences in approach and perspective between the Old and New left became defined and took on substance, and the structures of these organizations provided an organizational form for the early development of the New Left. The differences within and between these single-issue and multi-issue organizations, moreover, were not merely differences over the tactics of social change, but embodied the fundamentally different perceptions of reality held by the Old Left and New Left.

The changing character and focus of the civil-rights movement, and the experiments with single-issue and multi-issue organizing at the end of the fifties, are a necessary point of departure in attempting to understand the ingredients that went into the formation of a New Left in the nineteen-sixties. At the same time, however, the particular combination of those ingredients that came to characterize it as a *new* Left can only be understood in relation to the left that preceded it. The New Left has often been described as a break with the Old Left, but it was also a *response* to the Old Left. It was precisely because members of Old Left organizations often were active in these new efforts at dissent, and because they brought with them systematic and coherent analyses of how change should occur, that the new activists were forced to examine and confront the positions of the Old Left. The fact that the New Left adopted a different analysis and strategy was not some accident of history, but was a considered response to what they perceived to be the failures and limitations of the Old Left, and in order to understand that response it is first necessary to examine the broad outlines of the Old Left experience that shaped it. From an examination of that experience, and the implications of that experience for radical activity in the sixties, we may develop an understanding of one of the particular historical circumstances that conditioned the development of a theory and practice by a New Left.

2 Dissent in the Fifties

In the process of accommodation to the corporate way of life something has been lost. Perhaps what has been lost is no less than Youth itself–the restlessness, the discontent with things as they are, the seeking of new ways, new modes of existence, the rejection of old hypocrisies, the intense searching within and without–all these the corporation cannot understand and has no room for.

(Venture, April 1959)

For those who have grown up amidst the turbulent dissent of the nineteen-sixties, as well as for the generation that reached maturity during the great economic and political struggles of the thirties, the political climate of the decade following World War II must be difficult to comprehend. The postwar period witnessed the suppression and disintegration of the organized left in America, the decline of political activity among students, and a general suspension of critical political activity throughout American society.

The aftermath of world war was a time for reorganization in all the institutions of society. Families were reunited after four years of war, and set about building stable and secure futures; the economy converted from a total emphasis on war production to a mixture of defense and civilian production and sought new markets for expansion; and the political system, which had found a certain stability in wartime after the upheavals of the thirties, was faced with a resurgence of domestic problems.

The response to conditions of peace was not, however, a traumatic restructuring of social institutions. Instead, new enemies appeared on the international scene, forcing a continued emphasis on foreign policy and defense, and obscuring the dramatic changes taking place in the character of domestic life. The Soviet Union replaced the Fascists as the main threat to American interests, and, in 1949, China joined the ranks of former allies now confronting us as enemies. "Containing communism" became the central objective of US foreign policy. The fear of Communist regimes spreading to Europe and elsewhere, combined with a memory of the domestic strength communism had shown in the thirties, led to a new wave of repressive legislation governing political dissent, which culminated in the "McCarthy Era" of the late forties and early fifties. Discussion of political ideas that did not conform to official policy became a hazardous business.[1]

31

As the fifties came to an end, so, too, did the "generation of silence" spawned during the postwar years. The renewed interest in political activity did not take a uniform character, but developed in different ways and at different speed among different groups, with many aborted efforts along the way. When it did develop, moreover, it represented a break with the political and organizational continuity that had characterized the American left since the thirties.

The Consolidation of Labor

After two decades of bitter struggles during which "organized" labor grew in size, power, and legality, the years following World War II marked a time of consolidation in the trade union movement.[2] Leo Troy has estimated that there were about 12.1 million union members in the United States in 1945, comprising 22.4 percent of the civilian labor force. By 1953, union members comprised 25.7 percent of the labor force, but by 1957 the percentage had declined to about 24.5 percent,[3] and by 1966 had further declined to 22.7 percent. This decline in growth was partly a reflection of changes in the character of the labor force, but it also reflected important changes in the labor movement itself.

In a pioneering study of "white-collar" occupations, C. Wright Mills pointed out that by 1940 the "old middle class" of self-employed small entrepreneurs and farm owners was being replaced by a "new middle class" comprised of salaried white-collar workers, and that the life-styles and beliefs of these two groupings were quite different.[4] Nevertheless, during the first half of this century the composition of the labor force was fairly typical of industrial capitalism, with "blue-collar" workers employed in direct production comprising the bulk of the labor force. It was among these workers that the great union organizing drives of the thirties had taken place, and from them that the unions drew their strength. After World War II, however, this pattern began to change.

In 1950 blue-collar workers represented about 37.4 percent of the labor force, but by 1960 they had declined to about 36.3 percent, and by 1970 represented about 35.3 percent. During the same period, white-collar workers increased from 37.5 percent in 1950, to 43.1 percent in 1960, and reached about 48.3 percent in 1970.[5] Within the private sector alone, "nonproduction" workers increased sharply relative to total employment from 12.4 percent in 1950 to 16.1 percent in 1960, gradually increasing to 17.1 percent in 1969.[6] Employment in the public sector shows even sharper changes, and the growth in public vs. private sectors has accelerated the trend toward white-collar dominance of the labor force. While the causes and full implications of this change are the subjects of much debate (which

we will return to in later chapters), their implications for the labor movement are fairly obvious—and severe. For example, a very large number of
white-collar workers are employed by federal, state, or local governments,
where restrictions on union organizing and union activities are considerably more stringent than in the private sector. As late as 1970, white-collar
workers comprised only about 16 percent of all union members, and only
about 12 percent of white-collar workers were in unions.[7] These changes in
the labor force, which accelerated after World War II, constituted a tangi-
ble, structural obstacle to continued growth of the labor movement along
the same lines it had followed in the thirties and forties, and when this was
compounded by strong antilabor political problems, such as the Taft-
Hartley Act, the political character of the labor movement changed dramat-
ically.

Internally, the decade following the war was a time of merger in the
labor movement, and a time when Communists were expelled from leadership positions. The separate development of the American Federation of
Labor and the Congress of Industrial Organizations during the nineteen-
thirties had reflected the changing character of blue-collar occupations
during the first part of this century. As more and more workers were forced
into mass industrial settings, the traditional form of union organization
along "craft" lines became less meaningful than organization according to
the "industry" in which they worked, and this led to new unions organized
by industry. The older craft unions often resented this intrusion on their
power, and hostility between the two types of unions was often great.

In addition to different organizational forms, however, the split between the AFL and C' ɔ was a split over different approaches to political
activity. Where the AFL had always restricted itself to economic struggles
concerned strictly with worker self-interest, the CIO from the outset
adopted an activist political stance that attempted to better the social as
well as the economic condition of workers through political action. Communists and other left organizations whose primary objective was to build a
"class-conscious" working class were active in the organizing efforts to
build the CIO, and by the mid-forties a number of CIO unions had Communists in positions of leadership.[8]

The passage of the Taft-Hartley Act presented a direct challenge to the
labor movement: rid yourselves of the Communists in your ranks and gain a
secure legal position guaranteeing you a piece of the economic pie, or
defend the Communists in your ranks and risk losing even those rights you
won in the thirties. In 1948 and 1949, most unions (including the CIO
unions) adopted changes in their constitutions that made membership in the
Communist party ground for expulsion, and at the 1949 CIO convention a
new section was added to the constitution barring Communists from
leadership.[9]

This internal attack on the Communists, while accelerated by the Taft-Hartley Act, resulted from the isolation of the Communists within the labor movement caused by their constantly shifting line during the war, and by their opposition to the Marshall Plan and their support of the Henry Wallace campaign. It also reflected a power struggle within the CIO. In 1947, Walter Reuther was elected president of the powerful United Automobile Workers, and together with John L. Lewis's United Mineworkers and Philip Murray's United Steelworkers, this placed anti-Communist elements in control of the most powerful CIO unions. As Philip Taft observed:

Reuther's victory in 1947 was of the utmost importance to the trade-union movement and to the American people. It placed the United Automobile Workers Union solidly in the anticommunist camp. With Reuther, and his associates in full control, no weasling on the Marshall Plan or failure to support the program of the free world would be possible.[10]

In addition to purging Communists from leadership in their own unions, these CIO leaders began a systematic raiding of Communist-dominated unions which resulted in reduced membership and lessened influence for the "Red" unions. Together with the Taft-Hartley affidavit, these actions succeeded in virtually eliminating Communist influence in the labor movement within a few short years. It also removed the major obstacle to a reunification of the AFL and CIO.

Throughout the forties and early fifties, the major differences between the two federations gradually dwindled. Both now had a vested interest in continued economic expansion and a recognized role in guiding that expansion. The differences over political action converged toward a middle ground, when the AFL (frightened by its inability to block Taft-Hartley) for the first time created a separate political department, and the CIO turned toward conventional political activity (including withdrawal from the Communist-dominated World Federation of Trade Unions). Both federations supported US policy in the Korean War, and in December of 1950 agreed to create a joint United Labor Policy Committee to coordinate labor relationships with government during the war.

With the withdrawal of the United Mineworkers from membership in either federation, and the death of the presidents of both the AFL and CIO within eleven days of each other in 1952, the last personality conflicts blocking the way to reunification were ended, and the road to merger was opened. The policy of raiding unions of the opposite federation had proven costly and largely unproductive, while the difficulties presented by the Taft-Hartley Act urged cooperation. Within a few months of the ascension of George Meany to the presidency of the AFL and of Walter Reuther to the presidency of the CIO, meetings aimed at reunification began, and in

December of 1955, the merger was achieved, combining the economic emphasis of the AFL with an emphasis on political action through a Committee on Political Education.

The differences in social philosophy between the AFL and CIO, reflected in the personalities of Meany and Reuther, were not eliminated by the merger; indeed, in the late sixties Reuther led the UAW out of the AFL-CIO. Nevertheless, after the expulsion of the Communists, their differences were sufficiently less than their common interests to make joint efforts possible and to create the largest organization of labor in American history, representing more than 17 million workers in 1965. The long-run significance of this consolidation of labor after World War II is—even now—a matter of dispute, but the fact that it was, politically, an anti-Communist consolidation made its immediate impact on the organized left a devastating impact. It took away from the Communist left an organized base in the constituency that it looked to for progressive change, and the consequences of this loss were felt throughout the non-Communist left as well.

The Reorganization of the Left

For the organizations that comprised the American left, the end of war abroad marked the beginning of a war at home. As the United States emerged from the wreckage of World War II, a stronger power than ever before, the situation of the left grew desparate in the extreme. During the economic chaos of the thirties organizations like the Communist party and the Socialist party had grown in numbers and influence as their critique of the inherent evils of capitalism seemed borne out by the daily sufferings of millions of working people. The pioneering efforts by these organizations to organize the unorganized had given them bases of real power in the trade union movement, and for the Communists the example of the Soviet Union gave flesh to their vision of a socialist America. Everywhere, the "old order" seemed to be failing.[11]

In the aftermath of World War II, however, the left found itself facing a stronger and united opposition. Although production declined somewhat in postwar years, it never approached the low point of the Depression, and profit levels continued to rise. As the economy proved stable and provided both jobs and goods for a people weary of conflict, the massive economic discontent that marked the thirties failed to reappear. Indeed, those very forces that—through their excesses—had brought about the Depression, and had opposed the social welfare programs of the New Deal, now claimed credit for those programs and for the improved economic situation.[12]

What made the changed economic conditions so dangerous for the left politically, however, was the changing view of the Soviet Union. There had always been sharp criticism within the left about the lack of democracy under Soviet communism, but the claimed economic progress of the Soviet Union after the Bolshevik Revolution was offered as a positive example of what socialism could accomplish, and had been a major impetus to Communist recruiting. The Hitler-Stalin Pact just prior to World War II had dampened the appeal of the Soviet Union in the West, as had the changing line of Western Communist parties, which followed closely the foreign policy line of the USSR.[13] The final straw came with the establishment of pro-Soviet Communist regimes in Eastern Europe at the end of the war, which opened the way to a cold war that included an attack on the left at home. Almost overnight, the Soviet Union was transformed from a wartime ally into a dangerous enemy, and with the improved economic conditions in America, the lack of political democracy under communism became identified as the central feature of such regimes, rather than any potential ability to lift the standard of living of people under socialism.

The Turning Inward

This new set of circumstances both isolated and fragmented the American left. In the thirties, the main foreign threat was fascism, while at home "big business" and the very rich could be blamed for the plight of average people. The Soviet Union, despite its shortcomings, offered hope that a better life was possible. After the war, however, proponents of capitalism could argue that America offered a better life *plus* political freedom, while communism offered only totalitarian rule and slavish obedience to the Soviet Union.

In the thirties, the trade union movement had provided an organizational and political base for the organized left, while the economic crisis of American capitalism had made "liberalism" an ambivalent counterideology that sought to minimize differences with the left in order to broaden the appeal of New Deal programs. With the resurgence of the economy during wartime and the emergence of the cold war in the late forties, labor and liberal support for the left was stripped away. Although a great many New Deal liberals continued to insist (and suffered for their insistence) on the constitutional right of Communists and other political groups to organize and speak without restrictions, the expulsion of Communists from a base in the labor movement was accompanied by an ideological assault from a new kind of "cold-war liberalism." In 1949, for example, Arthur Schlesinger, Jr., a Harvard professor, leader of the liberal Americans for Democratic

Action, and historian of the New Deal, bluntly warned of the danger from the left:

> I have deliberately given more space to the problem of protecting the liberal faith from Communism than from reaction; not because reaction is the lesser threat, but because it is the enemy we know whose features are clearly delineated for us. . . . It is perhaps our very absorption in this age-old foe which has made us fatally slow to recognize the danger on what we certainly thought was our Left.[14]

New Deal liberalism, which had arisen in response to the failure of earlier laissez-faire ideology, had all along been concerned with saving capitalism by controlling its internal tendencies toward excess; with the merger of New Deal domestic emphases and cold war foreign policies, the new cold war liberalism was ready to take on the challenge from the left. Beginning with the labor movement, a series of legislative and judicial actions—often supported and sponsored by "liberal" congressmen —placed severe restraints on political activity by Communists and created a climate in which dissenting views of any sort were suspect. The effect on the Communist party was catastrophic, as its leaders were jailed and its members driven underground, and the decline in membership it experienced throughout the fifties was testimony to the effectiveness with which the old order had resisted the challenge of the Communist left. The decline was also, of course, a result of the continuing turmoil within the communist world. The Twentieth Party Congress in the Soviet Union; Hungary; and the emerging split between Russia and China—all these events had repercussions within the American Communist party, and led to many resignations and expulsions.

The repression of the Communists also created severe internal strains within the organized left. As the liberal and labor "progressives" turned against the Communists, organizations like the Socialist party were faced with a crisis. Should they support the right of Communists to speak freely and organize, and thereby risk incurring the wrath of the liberal and labor elements themselves, or should they join in the chorus of condemnation in the hope that these elements would rally to "democratic socialism" as an alternative? Given the history of hostility between the Socialists and Communists, as well as the former's genuine belief that Stalin's purges (and the refusal of the American Communist party to criticize them) were intolerable by any humane standards, it was not surprising that they chose to join in the attacks.[15] What was surprising was how quickly anticommunism on the left became as uncritical as anticommunism on the right. Norman Thomas, the perennial Socialist party candidate for president, went so far as to argue that the Communists had no right to civil liberties except as warranted by, "careful judgment of the immediacy of the peril the Communist Party creates and the practicality of any particular measure against it."[16]

Even more striking was the foreign policy position of the Socialist party. The proud "party of Debs," which had once obtained a million votes for its presidential candidate, by the late forties was scarcely distinguishable from the left of the Democratic party. Its foreign policy, moreover, was little different from that of the State Department, and in 1950 supported sending US troops to Korea.[17]

The sharp split between the foreign policy positions of the Communists and Socialists (with the former supporting the Soviet Union and the latter supporting the US) did not carry over in the same degree to analyses of domestic problems. Both retained a central focus on the need to organize the "industrial proletariat" by gaining converts in trade unions, an emphasis rooted in a belief that the "working class" was the agency for progressive change. In the economic conditions of the fifties, however, both seemed to accept a view that American capitalism had "stabilized" and averted the domestic collapse that seemed imminent in the thirties. Both concentrated their attention primarily on foreign policy issues and ignored the changing composition of the labor force, refrained from attacking the growing alliance of "big labor" and big business, and largely refrained from any analysis of the growing bureaucratization and decline of internal democracy within the trade union movement.

Others on the left did pay more attention to such issues, however. Although the major split within the left during the fifties was between the Communists and everyone else, there were also divisions in the non-Communist left. Ever since the thirties the American left had included, beside Communists and Socialists (social-democrats), a significant number who considered themselves followers of Leon Trotsky. The original split between the Communists and the Trotskyists was over the issue of whether socialism could be achieved in one country before a worldwide socialist revolution, but over the years new points of difference arose within the Trotskyist ranks, resulting in additional splinter organizations.[18] By the early fifties, there were two "major" Trotskyist organizations vying for influence with the Communists and Socialists. One was the Socialist Workers party, the "mainline" organization with origins in the original split. The SWP was highly critical of Stalin and the development of bureaucratic control in the Soviet Union, but supported the Communist camp in its struggle with the United States.[19] During the fifties, however, the SWP was not a major factor in the internal struggles of the left, and remained marginal to the developments of that period.

The Independent Socialist League played a far more central role in those struggles. Founded as the Workers party in a split with the SWP after the Soviet invasion of Finland, this organization espoused a "third camp" political position that combined equal condemnation of the United States and the Soviet Union, and called for the creation of an independent movement of revolutionary socialists:

We characterize the Soviet Union as one of the two war camps, as an expansionist power that uses the atmosphere of war and crisis to tie its oppressed peoples to their backward regime. . . .

The United States is the other war camp. . . . It is the last bulwark of Western imperialism. . . .

The third camp is the concept of a force independent of both imperialist camps. It need not necessarily be a socialist force, but it represents that section of the world which is not integrated into the war machines of either of the two camps.[20]

Led by Max Schachtman, one of the founders of the American Communist party (later expelled as a Trotskyist), the importance of the ISL in the fifties derived primarily from the ability of its student wing—the Young Socialist League—to infiltrate and gain control of the youth wing of the Socialist party. The third camp position it espoused later found adherents among the early activists of the New Left and, more immediately, among the pacifist wing of the non-Communist left.

Many smaller organizations belonged to the "political" left in the fifties, but the only one to play any significant role was the League for Industrial Democracy. The LID was an "educational" organization that included socialists and liberals, and as the sixties began, the student department of the LID became the base of the Students for a Democratic Society, but throughout the fifties the adult LID aligned itself with anti-Communist liberals to support US foreign policy. Many of its members were active in the Congress of Cultural Freedom, whose ties to the CIA were later exposed by Christopher Lasch.[21]

Pacifism and the Left

No discussion of the American left in the fifties is complete without some mention of the pacifists. Although they maintained their own organizations distinct from those of the Communists and Socialists, the overlap in membership was often great, and the pacifist critique of American society focused on many of the same features as the more "political" left organizations. Unlike the political left, however, the pacifist critique was rooted in primarily moral issues. While groups like the Fellowship of Reconciliation and American Friends Service Committee based their pacifism in religious convictions, other groups such as the War Resistors League tended to be more secular and humanistic. In general, however, the pacifists agreed on several fundamental propositions about how to act out pacifist convictions:

first, that only persons who actually withdrew support from the use of military force would be taken seriously; second, that direct action and civil disobedience could force people who witnessed or read about them to think about their implications; and third, that actions of personal sacrifice could lead to a dialogue with other citizens on the merits of the pacifist position.[22] While their numbers were never great, this commitment to action on the part of the pacifists provided most of the visible opposition to the status quo during the postwar years.

The guiding figure among the pacifists was the Reverend A.J. Muste. During the thirties, Muste had played a central role in bringing liberal and religious elements together with more traditional left organizations, and whatever influence the pacifists had during the fifties was largely a testimony to his personality. After heading the FOR throughout the forties, Muste resigned in 1953 and, together with Bayard Rustin, founded *Liberation* magazine in 1956. *Liberation* quickly became the main voice for pacifist thinking in the late fifties, but its influence reached far beyond a narrow pacifist base. For a time, several leaders of the newly emerging African states, such as Tom M'boya and Kenneth Kaunda, were in closer contact with Bayard Rustin and *Liberation* than they were with the US State Department, and the magazine was one of the first journals with a predominantly white readership to treat seriously and in depth the struggle for equality by southern blacks.[23] In 1958, Muste formed the Committee for Nonviolent Action, which organized civil disobedience against militarism and nuclear testing, and the CNVA played a key role in initiating the new "peace movement" that spread at the end of the decade.

In a decade that witnessed the decline and disintegration of most organizations of the adult left, the contribution of the pacifists was not so much in the numbers of people they involved, as in their refusal to give in to the hysteria of McCarthyism and their continuing insistence that the real enemy of the left was not other "leftists," but a system of militarism and racism that dominated power in America. Their absolute moral positions and tendency toward anarchism might have proven a hindrance during a real struggle for political power, but during a period when the crisis for the left was one of "faith" in its goals and a willingness to act, these same characteristics were a source of strength.

The Young Left in the Fifties

The *future* potential of political organizations is, in part, determined by their ability to recruit new members and to hold their allegiance over time. By the mid-fifties, the organized adult left was in a state of near total collapse, but the over-all situation of the youth and student left was, if anything, worse. The Communist party had established a new youth wing, the Labor Youth League, in 1950, but it never attracted much support beyond those who came from party backgrounds, and was finally dissolved in 1957.[24] The LYL was clearly a relic of earlier times, and its approach was out of tune with the prevailing mood of the period. Some of the flavor of its analysis was reflected in a "Statement of Principles":

It recognizes the working class as the source of progress in the modern world, as the defender of the democratic traditions of our country, as the force capable of assuring lasting peace. . . .

The League stands against the big business tycoons whose system exists by war and misery. It opposes Wall Street's preparations for a third world war. . . .

The League stands for friendship between the U.S.A. and the U.S.S.R. as the cornerstone of lasting peace. . . .

The League works for the forging of unbreakable solidarity between Negro and white youth, in the conviction that this unity is indispensable to the fight for peace.[25]

Whatever potential the LYL might have had for growth was undermined by several factors. First, it was created just as the Korean War was beginning, and at a time when the hysteria against communism was reaching a peak. The Communist party was under attack on all fronts and unable to provide major assistance to the youth organization. Moreover, the practical basis for its appeal rested in a call for "a vigorous defense of the economic rights and interests of working youth, threatened by mounting unemployment and developing economic crisis"[26]—a condition that was changing at that very moment.

Unemployment among young people, traditionally higher than the over-all unemployment rate, had, indeed, soared in the years following World War II, but between 1950 and 1953 (largely because of the war), it dropped to a new low of slightly more than 6 percent.[27] At the same time, the proportion of young people going to college began a dramatic increase, and these changes helped to remove any sense of impending economic crisis among young people at the same time that the official reaction against Communism reached a peak.

Members of the LYL were active in student government and student newspapers on a few large campuses, and the organization did maintain a certain "culture" of radicalism among its members during a difficult period for the left.[28] Some of these students went on to play important roles in the development of a New Left in the sixties, but the Communists lost the opportunity to play a direct organizational role in that development when, after disbanding the LYL, the Communist party decided that the time was not ripe for a new student and youth organization.[29]

Besides the LYL, the major youth organizations of the left during the fifties were the Young People's Socialist League (youth wing of the Socialist party), the Young Socialist League (youth wing of the ISL), and the Student League for Industrial Democracy. The last of these, although it maintained a paper membership of about two hundred during the fifties, had practically no influence on developments within the left. It did sponsor occasional lectures and debates on campuses, and its leaders attended international conferences, but it was not until it went through a dramatic internal reorganization at the end of the decade that the SLID was really counted as part of the left.[30] One of the leaders of SLID in the fifties summed up the organization's role:

When I first joined SLID, in 1954, its total active membership was in the dozens. Of course, figures were inflated by leaving people on membership lists, allowing older, part-time students to stay on "at large," etc. . . . .
Only a few of us in SLID thought of ourselves as socialists of any kind. Most of our members were liberals, though . . . they were willing to belong to a group that was meant to be a coalition of the left.[31]

The Young People's Socialist League and the Young Socialist League were considerably more active, but most of their activity was directed to internal faction fights. Throughout its history, the YPSL was periodically embroiled in attempts by various Trotskyist groups to win over its members, and each time such efforts succeeded, the adult SP would suspend the youth group and start to rebuild the organization with "reliable" youth.[32] In the fifties, the "third camp" politics of the ISL and its youth affiliate, as well as its willingness to fight for civil liberties for *all* political groups, found considerable support among YPSL members, and in 1953, a majority of the YPSL leadership shifted to support of the YSL positions. This led to censure by the Socialist party and the withdrawal of the youth group from the SP—and along with it went several key leaders, including Michael Harrington.[33] For the remainder of the decade, sometimes under the YPSL name and sometimes as the YSL, the only overtly "socialist" young left was dominated by the "Schachtmanite"[34] perspective which, in addition to a third-camp position on foreign policy and an emphasis on civil liberties, advocated the formation of an independent Labor party as the main short-range goal of an American left. Even those who remained in the SP-YPSL after the split disagreed less with the political positions of the YSL than they did with its manipulative organizational practice of "raiding" other organizations.[35]

Toward Socialist Realignment

The declining numerical strength of the left during the fifties—which accel-

erated after Khruschev's denunciation of Stalin at the Twentieth Party
Congress, and after the invasion of Hungary—led to attempts during the
latter part of the decade to pull the splintered left back together. In late 1956
and early 1957, a major debate within the youth wings of both the SP and the
ISL centered on the need for "socialist realignment" and "socialist unity."
The major considerations in this debate were spelled out in a YSL resolution early in 1957:

Unlike other groups, the independent socialist tendency does not feel that our
organizations as such constitute the "Socialist Movement" of the United
States. . . .

Instead, we have oriented towards the creation of a labor party as the next important progressive step in the development of the American workers. Such a development will precede the development of a socialist working class. . . . Our
tasks in connection with a labor party will be to support it . . . and together with
other socialists, to constitute a socialist wing in it which would aim at winning the
party as a whole to socialist program and a socialist leadership. . . .

For many years the Communist Party had a large hold . . . on radical sentiment in
the United States . . . the recent earth-shaking developments in the Stalinist world .
. . . have once and for all eliminated the CP from being able to play this role. . . .
A new broad socialist movement could establish itself as the center of radicalism
and socialism in the United States . . . whereas none of the existing sects can do
so. . . .

Our interest in socialist unity is based precisely on these considerations, and mainly
on the view that it would produce a movement which in numerical strength and
influence would far transcend the arithmetic addition of those sects participating in
the merger. . . . Because of its name, tradition, history, and general character, the
Socialist Party can play a key role in the creation of a new socialist movement. . . .

There are a series of "historical" issues which divide the traditions of the SP, the
ISL, and the YSL. . . . But we do not believe that they should be a bar to joint
activity in a single organization. What is crucial is that the organization be in
agreement on the political questions . . . that we stand for civil liberties for all, for
an extension and deepening of democracy. . . .

The independent socialist tendency does not make changes in the programs or
leadership of the Socialist Party conditions for [merger]. On the contrary, it is ready
to unite with the Socialist Party as it stands today.[36]

At the July 1957 convention of the independent Socialist League, the
delegates voted to merge with the Socialist party, and a year later the SP
voted to accept the merger.[37] Support for the merger within the SP largely
centered in the YPSL and in a "left-wing opposition" in the SP, both of
which believed that the merger would strengthen the third-camp position
and lead to independent political organizing, but what transpired was rather
different from these expectations. Schachtman, Harrington, and the others
who came into the SP with the merger argued that the way to build a labor
party was by "realigning" the Democratic party, and that the strategy of
the left should be to forge an alliance between civil rights, peace, and labor

forces within the Democratic party that would force the Dixiecrats out. The realignment resolution passed the 1960 convention of the SP, and the party decided not to run its own candidate in the forthcoming presidential election.[38]

The focus on realignment and socialist unity did not, however, lead to a dramatic growth in the numerical or political strength of the left, and by 1960 the left was "regrouped," but weaker than ever. The Communists had no formal youth movement, while the youth wing of the Socialist party was sharply divided between those who supported the realignment position and those who wanted an independent labor party. A section of the YSL refused to even go along with the merger, and joined with youth from the Socialist Workers party to compete with the new YPSL. In 1960, this group formed the Young Socialist Alliance, and although for many years it remained a tiny sect, in the later sixties it took a leading role in student protest against the war in Vietnam.[39]

The Remains of the Old Left

By any standards, the American left was in bad shape as a new decade dawned. While the organizations of the left waged intense, internecine warfare throughout the fifties, their numbers dwindled and grew minuscule in comparison with earlier times. In his excellent history of the New Left, James P. O'Brien estimates that only about 80,000 persons subscribed to as many as one radical journal during the fifties.[40] Compare this figure with the thirteen daily newspapers and 298 weeklies the Socialist party alone maintained during the first two decades of this century, and some sense of the enormity of the decline is apparent.[41] The fifties were a different age, and the numbers of activists could be counted in the tens and hundreds, rather than in the tens of thousands. As a new decade began, what remained was the remnants of an adult left, and no real young left. Those who had "survived" the fifties hardly imagined that a new upsurge of political protest was just around the corner, and the words of one youth leader of the YPSL in the late forties, who went on to leadership in the Socialist party, are probably typical of the attitude of the young left in the fifties:

The hope of any real change, in any near sense, was always denied us in the fifties. We were excited when we were together—we were young—about being Socialists, about changing the world; but there was no sense that we were, in fact, about to do that. . . . And if we wrote "Socialism in our time" on bathroom walls, it was an awfully youthful, naive optimism . . . I viewed, and I think most of us in my generation who were active viewed it as a holding operation. Things would change later, but there was no sense of being anywhere close to touching power in any sense at all.[42]

The left at the end of the fifties was "old." It was old in the sense that its adult members had reached political maturity in the thirties and forties, and it had no youth or student movement during the fifties to give it energy or vision. It was also old in the sense that its analysis and vision were rooted in an America that was fast disappearing. Even as the adult organizations of the left battled each other for influence over a declining constituency, they all retained an analysis of the "industrial proletariat" and the progressive role of trade unions that ignored their own experience in the postwar decade and that was oblivious to the changing character of American capitalism. They saw only that capitalism had "stabilized," but they did not look behind that superficial reality to find out how and why it had done so. Confronted by a resurgent ideological struggle on the international scene between "communism" and the "free world," and faced with mounting domestic repression, the organized left was unable to sustain itself and to adapt to the new conditions of American society. And to a new generation of students entering college at the end of the fifties, this Old Left appeared as a relic of some earlier era which had failed in its promise and which offered no perspective or program for the problems they faced. It remained for new forces not embroiled in the internal struggle of the fifties to sense the changes that had taken place, and to begin—hesitantly at first—to develop new forms of struggle in the decade ahead.

Rumblings in the Silent Generation

If the fifties were a time of stagnation and decline for most of the youth groups of the organized left, few college students of the day were probably aware that these groups even existed. It was not so much that college students joined actively in the anti-Communist hysteria of the period, as that they avoided political discussion entirely. "Silence" seemed the apt description of this generation of students, and throughout the early fifties popular journals noted—often unfavorably—this strange quiescence.[43]

It was not, of course, that college students during the early fifties had *no* interests, but rather that their priorities were different from what they had been in the thirties. This was the first generation in two decades to be plagued neither with economic crisis, nor—after Korea—with war abroad, and they seemed determined to make the most of their situation. One survey of eleven campuses in 1952 found that most rated "a stable, secure future" even higher than they rated "a chance to earn a good deal of money," and they were not inclined to jeopardize their chances for security.[44] Other surveys at the time found them generally satisfied with their education[45] and fearful of discussing current social problems.[46]

Beneath the quiet surface, however, there were a few discordant notes, even in the early fifties. The same survey that found students generally satisfied with their education also found agreement with the assertion that "charges of 'production line' teaching methods are justified."[47] Another survey in 1952 found that the vast majority of students agreed "If I had the opportunity to stay out of military service, I would certainly take advantage of it."[48] Such an attitude was, of course, compatible with a desire to progress unimpeded toward a secure future, but it also indicated that the Korean War was viewed differently from the earlier war against fascism. None of these discordant notes found expression in organized forms of political dissent, but together with more "apathetic" attitudes they indicated a prevailing mood on campus that was not so much one of total agreement with the repressive political climate, as it was one of a withholding of judgment. In the words of one observer, the college student generation of the early fifties exhibited "an almost excessive balance, an overpowering care not to commit its emotions too deeply to anything."[49]

The National Student Association

Throughout the early fifties, what little political activity there was by students mostly centered (as was the case with the young left) on foreign policy issues. The only national organization of students with any political significance was the National Student Association, an association of student governments formed to counter the international activities of students in Communist countries.

In 1946, an international student conference held in Prague had given birth to the International Union of Students, whose stated aims were to act as a clearing house for news about students in different countries and to act as an advocate for issues of concern to students. The IUS was, however, clearly dominated by Communist students and primarily supported by Communist countries, and the twenty-five American students who attended the Prague conference returned home hoping to create an American student organization, nationwide in scope and representative in character, which could compete with the well-organized European student organizations. They held two conferences in the US during the next year, and at the second one (at the University of Wisconsin) the National Student Association of the USA was created.[50] Although the NSA was never a mass membership organization with which students could closely identify, it did function fairly successfully as *the* representative of American students until it was racked by disclosures of CIA influence in the late sixties. After its formation, the NSA joined with other non-Communist student organizations from Western Europe in sponsoring a series of "international Student

Conferences" which served as a "free world" counterpart to the IUS conferences.[51]

During the early fifties the NSA was viewed by the US government as an important weapon in the cold war with communism, and beginning in 1952 the organization started to receive substantial funding for its international activities from the Central Intelligence Agency.[52] The NSA-supported foreign student leaders wishing to study in the US, and for four years during the Algerian revolution served as a channel for CIA money to Algerian student leaders.[53] William T. Dentzler, a former president of NSA and one of the chief architects of its international role, clearly summarized the importance of the organization as a counter to Communist influence among students:

The efforts of the State Department abroad often are labeled as "government propaganda," but American people abroad acting as just plain persons who honestly are interested in peace, liberty, and democracy, and in helping foreign groups, can do a tremendous amount of good for the free world as they operate free from the label of "agent of the State Department."[54]

The international activities of the NSA were, however, little known among students at large—and probably of less interest. The main domestic activity of the organization was the Annual Student Congress, which brought together student government leaders and editors of student newspapers from around the country to discuss political issues. Although a few "leftist" students from large campuses went to these gatherings and were involved in NSA through their local involvement in student government and campus newspapers, the majority of student governments seemed less concerned with major political issues of national concern than with local campus social issues. An NSA survey in 1955 showed that at schools that had fraternities, 84 percent of the student government posts were held by fraternity members, and there seems to have been a tradition of contests between fraternities for control of student governments.[55] Thus, in the fifties, the domestic activities of the NSA were largely subordinate to its international activities, and only with the development of the civil-rights movement and the rise of a New Left in the early sixties did the focus and function of the organization begin to shift to domestic political issues.

The Beats

Instead of developing political forms of protest, disaffection with the emerging corporate "American way of life" in the fifties was primarily expressed in "cultural" rebellion. The spokesmen for this cultural protest were not, themselves, students, but were older writers and artists. The real

"Beat" movement they celebrated in poem and verse had taken place in the late forties and early fifties, but toward the end of the fifties the poems of Allan Ginsberg and Lawrence Ferlingetti and the novels of Jack Kerouac found an audience on the periphery of the great universities.[56]

Coffeehouses featuring folk music, poetry readings, drugs, and sex sprang up at places like Berkeley, Chicago, the City University of New York, Ann Arbor, and even at schools like Oberlin, Antioch, Northwestern, and Cornell. The Beat influence combined a rejection of prevailing standards about sex and drugs with an "existential" and even mystical challenge to positivist emphases on "facts" and "reason." It represented a turning inward away from a society that seemed to have all of life programmed in advance, and a search for new frontiers in the "soul" where none existed in society.[57] The Beat movement was, however, only a one-sided movement of negation, which could—at best—offer an escape from the world, but not any change in the social institutions that created the desire to escape. For the generation of college students entering in the late fifties, the Beat culture often provided a beginning of the quest for an authentic identity, but something more was needed to establish that identity.

The End of an Era

The world of a student entering college in 1960 was probably more different from that of his 1945 counterpart than was the latter's from a student of 1912. On the international scene, old enemies had become new friends, and old allies confronted us as enemies. The "labor movement" of the thirties had become "big labor" in the fifties, while the ideological appeal of socialism that had guided political activity in the thirties had been transformed into a Stalinist nightmare that repelled men from political thought. It is, perhaps, no wonder that a generation of intellectuals whose interests and analytical skills had been developed in the economic and political conditions of the thirties should have found in postwar America an "end of ideology." The issues that had moved them had, indeed, been either settled or eliminated by the changes that had occurred. The political ideologies that had won their allegiance in earlier times not only seemed to be intellectually bankrupt, but also to have been hopelessly betrayed by those who claimed to follow them.

What they did not see (and perhaps could not see) was that the very changes that had settled those earlier issues produced new issues and demanded new ideologies. The fifties marked one-half of a transition in the American left, the half that involved the decline and disintegration of social and political relationships which were part of what was dying away in American society. The sixties would witness the other half of the transition, the emergence into visibility of social and political relationships that had been growing within the old order. But although the Old Left was part of what was dying away, it still had to be confronted by those who would create a New Left, even if the form of that confrontation was one of total negation of what had gone before. In that meeting of the Old and New Left, an important part of the character and identity of the New Left would be shaped.

3

No Tests East or West

I said that the Old Left, despite its decline and apparent "failure," confronted those who sought to build a New Left as a theory and practice toward which they had to define their relationship; the New Left could not simply ignore the old. To understand why this was so, let us examine one of those aborted organizational efforts that *might* have, provided the organizational foundation of a New Left, but did not. Many accounts of the New Left, in attempting to identify those elements by which it differed from an older left, have emphasized the moral rather than the "political" sentiments behind its actions, the ad hoc and independent character of its organizations, its "middle-class" student composition, and similar characteristics. If these were the only important distinctions, then the Student Peace Union (rather than the SDS) might lay claim to being the first national organization of the New Left.

The Student Peace Union was formed in April of 1959 as a "regional student peace organization" in the Midwest. For several months prior to that time a young staff worker for the American Friends Service Committee, Ken Calkins, had been meeting with students from seven or eight campuses in the Chicago area in an effort to establish campus groups relating to the peace concerns of the AFSC. In addition to his position with the AFSC, Calkins was a pacifist member of the Fellowship of Reconciliation and the Committee for Nonviolent Action, and a member of the Socialist party. Calkins wanted to create a broader regional organization, similar to Student SANE but with different politics, that could appeal to nonpacifist students, and the Student Peace Union grew out of this effort.

The growth of the SPU was phenomenal over the next several years, and from 1960 to 1962 it dominated what there was of student activity on the left. By the end of October 1959, the SPU had members on twenty-one campuses in Illinois, Wisconsin, and Indiana. By June of 1960, it had over 150 members on fifty campuses around the country and was on its way to becoming a national organization. In the next two years, membership rose to some two thousand, and by the summer of 1963 the organization claimed more than four thousand members.[1] The budget of the organization (raised primarily from contributions) grew from about $1000 in 1959-60 to well over $22,000 in 1961-62, and the organization published a *Bulletin* containing chapter reports and analytical articles on foreign policy that reached a circulation of more than eight thousand copies by 1963. In February of

1962, the SPU helped organize a demonstration against nuclear testing that brought some eight thousand students to Washington.

The demise of the SPU was equally spectacular. By June of 1964, membership had declined drastically, the budget was down a third from the previous year, and at its annual convention that summer the organization voted to dissolve. The main reason for the sudden decline was, unquestionably, the signing of a partial test ban treaty on nuclear weapons by the US and the Soviet Union in November of 1963, which removed the main issue that had fueled the SPU's growth. In the process of the growth and decline of the SPU, however, were contained some central lessons and experiences that shaped the later development of the New Left.

The Politics of the SPU

At its first annual conference in 1959, the SPU adopted a Statement of Purpose that reflected the religious and pacifist background of the students with whom Ken Calkins had been working:

The Student Peace Union is an organization of students and young people who, believing that war can no longer be used to settle international differences, have joined together to study the causes of war and seek constructive alternatives to the present international situation, to study the techniques of reconciliation and to work to build a society which will know no more war, which will suffer no individual or group to be exploited by another, and which will assure to all the means for realizing the best possibilities of life.[2]

The only condition for membership in the SPU was agreement with this statement, and local chapters were autonomous in carrying out their own programs and recruitment. In 1960 the organization sponsored a Midwest speaking tour by David McReynolds of the War Resistors League, and cosponsored the Easter peace walk in Chicago. Although the overriding concern of the organization was the nuclear arms race and the need for disarmament, it also concerned itself with other foreign policy issues affecting war and peace, and early issues of the *Bulletin* carried articles on the developing crisis in Laos, the southern sit-ins, and an anti-ROTC protest at Berkeley.

The combination of moral and political motivations that became characteristic of the New Left in its fullest development were evident in the composition of the SPU. Very rapidly, three main "political" tendencies could be discerned among both the leadership and the membership of the organization. One group's primary affiliation was with the Young People's Socialist League, which encouraged its members to join the SPU as early as 1960.[3] At the time, the YPSL was in the midst of a vigorous internal struggle between those who wanted to accept the "realignment" strategy of the Socialist party and those who wanted to press for an independent labor party not tied to the Democratic party. Since the University of Chicago YPSL chapter was dominated by the "labor party tendency," and the national office of the SPU was in Chicago, it was this group which was most active in SPU activities.[4] Perhaps the briefest statement of the political perspective this group presented was given by one member running for election to the SPU National Council: "In terms of political viewpoint, I am for unilateral disarmament, but I am not a pacifist. I am a Marxist-Leninist, whose political activity centers around the overthrow of capitalism."[5]

The second major political grouping in the SPU was the radical pacifists (often anarchopacifists) who were drawn to the SPU because it seemed to offer the possibility of reaching a broader audience than did the existing pacifist organizations. They also were more interested in building a mass movement of protest than in the "symbolic" actions favored by adult pacifists. Another youth running for the National Council characterized the political views of this group:

I am still a radical pacifist, though I see SPU's activities and campus-community contact/discussion base as more meaningful than CNVA's overly "symbolic" focus. I am not a Marxist, of any brand, though I accept much of his analysis but tend to place more importance on cultural and anthropological rather than on economic factors as the primary basis for any really meaningful changes in men's relationships.[6]

Certainly the most numerous "groupings" within the SPU, however, were those students without other political affiliations who were drawn to it because of the issues it raised. The Student Peace Union, although it often began with only three or four members on campus, quickly became visible as a vehicle for students who were opposed to nuclear testing, but who had no sharply defined political views that would lead them toward more "traditional" left organizations. One such student, who later became a member of the SPU National Steering Committee, recalled her early involvement:

It was in 1958 or 1959 that I heard about the Easter peace march that happened in Chicago. . . . When Margie came and said that there is this march going on against bombs, it struck me as eminently sensible that one of the things that one should do if one were opposed to the bomb was get out and have a march. . . . And then the next year comes around, and it dawns on me that the peace march is coming to town at Eastertime, and no one would go unless I told them. So that year I got a little group of people together and got them to march the distance . . . and I got to meet people—this is where I found out about the Student Peace Union.[7]

By the time of the National Planning Committee meeting in August of 1960, YPSL members dominated the leadership of the SPU, and this led to a change in the Statement of Purpose reflecting the "third camp" politics of the YPSL. This was further strengthened in 1962, when the statement was again changed:

Because both East and West have pursued foreign policies which are not in the interests of their own people or the people of the world and because both bear major responsibility for the cold war, the Student Peace Union believes that the peace movement must act independently of both East and West, must apply the same standard of criticism to both, and must seek new and creative means of achieving a free and peaceful society.[8]

Also, in 1962, the organization began to broaden its political demands to include such items as the withdrawal of support from dictatorships and support for the right to self-determination for all countries. This trend continued throughout 1962, and in November the SPU organized protests against the blockade of Cuba (at the same time that it criticized the "Stalinization" of Cuba). At the 1963 convention, a statement on foreign policy was adopted that presented a lengthy analysis of the cold war and colonial revolutions, and a statement on civil rights was adopted which said, in part:

Peace and Freedom are morally and pragmatically inseparable. . . . There are significant differences between the peace movement and the civil rights movement. . . . More important, however, are the fundamental similarities of means, goals and opposition. . . . There is an intrinsic unity among these movements for social and political change: a lasting peace cannot be maintained so long as society permits individuals, groups or nations to be so oppressed that they feel their only recourse is to violence, revolution or war . . . .[9]

During 1963, the SPU maintained a field secretary who traveled the South trying to build SPU chapters and relating the foreign policy focus of the organization to the civil-rights issues, and he was eventually sentenced to a year in jail for his participation in demonstrations in Chapel Hill, North Carolina.[10] During the same year, the SPU organized demonstrations against the visit of Madame Ngu to the United States and began to call attention to the expanding war in Vietnam as a future crisis area.[11] Despite this broadening of issues, however, the organization remained almost entirely identified with foreign policy concerns. The detente between the Soviet Union and the United States took the heat out of the cold war, and with it went the sense of anxiety and urgency that had facilitated the rapid expansion of the SPU. Still, it might have survived and adapted itself to a new role in an emerging student left had it not been for the internal impact of the YPSL ties. It was here that the bankruptcy of the Old Left affected both the theory and practice of the organization and prevented it from becoming a vital force in creating a New Left.

The SPU and the Old Left

The numerical domination of the SPU leadership by YPSL members was not, in and of itself, the problem. Indeed, there was an important distinction among the YPSL members of the SPU between those whose primary "loyalty" was to the SPU and who had joined YPSL out of a belief that the problems confronting American society went beyond the issues of disarmament and foreign policy and required some form of "socialism" as a solution to these problems, and those whose primary loyalty was to the YPSL. The former constituted a majority of the SPU leadership, and for them, joining YPSL had seemed a natural outgrowth of their own political development. As one of them described her own decision to join YPSL:

And I remember, at the age of about fourteen or fifteen, the time that I first heard about what socialism was—and I heard about it in terms of Britain and Scandinavia—that the idea of welfare socialism really turned me on. . . . It had been completely obvious to me that our whole family had been screwed by having to pay for medical bills. . . .

At some point I got a membership form from the YPSL, and I just filled it out. . . . I had an understanding of socialism as . . . kind of tied up with the bomb thing—as "peace," and also a society where people would not be in need of basic necessities.[12]

A former national secretary of the SPU was far more direct in describing the attitude of those whose primary loyalty was to the SPU:

SPU—big, mass, growing important—and YPSL. . . . A handful of people who sit around and debate all the time—where socialism isn't on the agenda until some other time. . . . It was perfectly healthy, it seems to me, that people who spent their entire time working to build the SPU as an organization should feel some commitment to it—should feel that it would be somewhat of a betrayal . . . of all you have worked for if you suddenly say, "Well, my interest in this organization . . . was only because I'm in this [other] organization."[13]

Those whose primary loyalty was to the YPSL, on the other hand, viewed the SPU as a kind of "front group" for recruiting members. The single-issue SPU provided a pool of moralistic students who could be "educated" by YPSL members and recruited into the multi-issue YPSL. The result was a complex mixture of motivations, with some of the new recruits becoming organizers and supporters of the SPU within YPSL—as well as the reverse. A former national chairman of the SPU succinctly described the ambiguity of the relationship:

YPSL at that time was about three hundred people total. I think all these three hundred people were in the SPU and active in it—it was their major arena. And so you had people being fed YPSL stuff at the same time they were being fed SPU stuff, and they were simply all there in both groups because they were the radicals of their time—I mean they were interested in social issues. The SPU was where they did their activities—it was where they *did* things. . . . It served as a front group for YPSL . . . [but] people's commitment is where their activity is . . . . They were going on demonstrations that weren't YPSL demonstrations, they were SPU demonstrations.[14]

Because the YPSL was so closely involved with the SPU, the internal disputes of the former were often fought out in the SPU. This led, in 1962, to a sharp dispute between the Washington office of the SPU (controlled by "realignment" YPSLs) and the national office over the extent of SPU involvement in congressional elections that year.[15] The Washington office became heavily involved in these campaigns, while the Chicago leadership argued for an independent stance and continued emphasis on demonstrations. With the failure of most of the electoral efforts, this dispute subsided, but new divisions arose when the YPSL split apart in 1963. So much energy was expended within the YPSL on faction fights (there were some twenty-six "tendencies" in 1963) that the SPU had difficulty finding people to do the day-to-day work of the national office.[16] While the impact of these divisions on the SPU was certainly not as critical as the impact on the test-ban treaty, it did further weaken the organization's ability to adopt to the new international detente.

Despite the strains on the SPU caused by its ties to the YPSL, the different political strains within the organization could agree on a "third camp" political position. For the pacifists, this position grew out of an anarchist and moralist tradition that put them always at odds with the compromises that power necessitated, regardless of the form of the political system. For the hard-core YPSLs, it grew out of certain historical events in the development of the left, particularly the persecution of Trotskyists by Communists, and Stalin's terror. For the newer activists, the third camp position was compatible with the unquestioned anticommunism instilled in them during the fifties.

The issue of anticommunism was central, though behind the scenes, in the SPU, and its resolution within the organization lay somewhere between the explicit "exclusionary" practice of the non-Communist Old Left, and the "nonexclusionary" principle later followed by the New Left. The only condition for membership was agreement with the Statement of Purpose, and although this did not formally prevent Communists from joining, the YPSL leaders acted on the assumption that pro-Communist students could not honestly accept the third-camp position elaborated in the statement. Thus, while it represented a moderation of the practice of formally excluding Communists, its practical effect was much the same. Moreover, overt hostility to Communists was manifest in the relations of the SPU to other organizations, particularly to Student SANE. In 1971, for example, the rapid growth of a student peace movement led some of the adult left organizations to encourage unity between Student SANE and the SPU. The response of the SPU leadership to these overtures left no doubt as to their attitude toward cooperation with Communists, and this position was spelled out in a letter from the SPU national secretary to David McReynolds (who acted as "mediator" on behalf of the adult groups):

As far as the student peace movement in the U.S. goes, I believe and I think the point should be made, that the SPU is the only genuine national student peace group in the country today. Any attempt to build other peace groups is a sectarian approach since SPU is broad enough to encompass all *legitimate, honest* peace activity. . . .

My basic objection to Student SANE is that they are not critical enough of both the U.S. and Russian foreign policy . . . the official politics of SANE make it too easy for the "Russians" to function in the organization. . . . It seems to me that the socialists and the pacifists are committed to SPU. Student SANE *does* have a "Russian problem." [17]

The same writer, responding to an attempt within the YPSL to encourage the merger, was even more explicit in his denunciation:

I think it is evident that a large portion of the leadership of Student SANE is Stalinist. . . . Further, I believe it can be shown that most Student SANE locals that identify with the National are locally dependent on CP cadre for their existence. [18]

Thus, despite its apparent openness to any members in agreement with the Statement of Purpose, there was little attempt to hide the anticommunism of the leadership, an anticommunism that grew out of, and reflected, the traditional hostility between the YPSL and the Communist party. Not too surprisingly, this hostility was reciprocated by the Communists, and a letter from an SPU member at Oberlin College gives some of the flavor of this mutual antagonism in describing his conversation with a member of the Progressive Youth Organizing Committee (an organizing effort of the Communist party in 1961):

So this cool cat with dark glasses, name of Marvin, was eating with several of our guys. . . . Learned a lot [from him], like the SPU is splitting the peace movement, and it's really a shame that SLATE peace committee and SANE and SPU can't get together and "cooperate" . . . and why they (PYOC) want nothing to do with the YSA . . . and why the YPSL is so obstinate, and why SDS is all wrong on the peace question ("they say that there's an equal responsibility for the cold war, but really the socialist countries want peace") . . . .

On the interesting and exciting leaflet enclosed, this clean-cut all-American youth is billed as a civil-libertarian and an NSA boy, but somehow saw fit to omit his activities in Advance, and with the CCNY Marxist Discussion Group. [19]

The internal fights in YPSL and the hostility toward Communists were not the end of SPU's involvement with the Old Left. At the 1962 convention, and again at the 1963 convention, members of the Young Socialist Alliance (youth wing of the Socialist Workers party) attempted to gain control of the organization. The YSA was hostile to YPSL and the "Schachtmanites," and it sought to eliminate the explicit third-camp position from the Statement of Purpose.[20] The YSA did gain control of several local chapters, but was prevented from being seated at the convention largely as a result of opposition from non-YPSL delegates who had been steamrollered by the YSA in local chapter elections. Gail Paradise Kelly, national secretary at the time, claims that the YPSL delegates caucused and decided not to challenge the YSA credentials.[21]

The YSA also pushed strongly for the SPU to actively oppose the war in Vietnam, and it was that same opposition which in later years allowed the YSA to become a major force in the antiwar movement. At the 1963 SPU convention they proposed a resolution that read in part:

That this National Convention demands that the American government cease all military and political interference in the internal affairs of . . . South Vietnam. . . . We declare ourselves for the rights of self-determination for the people of South Vietnam.[22]

Because it was proposed by the YSA, this resolution was defeated at the convention, and although the SPU organized demonstrations against the war later in the year, the YSA largely withdrew from the organization. Thus, because of its size and visibility, the Student Peace Union became an arena in the early sixties for youth organizations of the Old Left to continue the internecine warfare of the fifties, and to attempt to recruit new members for their organizations. With YPSL members, who were deeply involved in these factional struggles, firmly in control of the leadership of the SPU, the internal disputes of the Old Left were guaranteed an importance out of proportion to their actual interest to the newer activists who were not members of the sect groups. Even more crucial was the attitude of the Old Left toward the possibility of building a left-oriented student movement from the SPU base.

The SPU: Between Old Left and New

From the outset, the SPU leadership recognized the desirability of, and need for, a left-oriented student movement. What prevented the SPU from becoming the umbrella organization for such a movement (as SDS later became) was the leadership's pessimistic assessment of the immediate prospects for such a movement and their limited conception of how such a movement could be built. The need for an *independent* student left, and the difficulties in achieving it, were detailed by David McReynolds during the debate on unity with Student SANE:

Youth—sociologically speaking—either have no decision-making power, and are simply involved in projects such as the AFSC sets up and in which case you can "control them" simply because they do not exist as a group. . . . Or, on the other hand, you have youth movements that are membership groups with policy powers. . . .

But in any group which sets up a student division and gives it policy-making power, and in which the adult and student groups are bound together by nothing more than an interest in peace or liberalism—an "interest in" rather than a coherent, shared set of principles—it is inevitable that very tense relationships will arise. And the history here in this country is organizational splits. . . .

In a sense what we aim at is Zengakuren (not its politics) in America, independent of adult groups but supported by some and so powerful, so shrewd in its practical organizational politics, that no other group can effectively counterorganize against it.[23]

The SPU leaders were, however, skeptical of the possibilities of such a movement being created in 1961, and in their views on this question the YPSL influence was clearly evident. They argued that no student left could develop in the absence of a credible adult left. Moreover, they argued that a student left could not develop a political ideology gradually, through reflection on experience, but must begin with a defined ideological stance:

In your letter you say that the "total lack of politics of SANE represents the real mood of most students." While I agree that it is true that most students lack politics, this does not mean that they are attracted to issue-oriented groups rather than to broad ideological groupings such as liberal clubs. In this context, they will only be repulsed by ideology if it is presented on a strong sectarian basis. Otherwise, ideology is what gives any depth to their experience in any isolated political activity today.[24]

A national cochairman of the SPU offered a similar analysis in an article in November of 1961. Arguing that "although a student movement is needed and wanted, it does not actually exist," he maintained that the only possibility of building such a movement was to center organizing efforts around specific issues in order to build commitment to a broad ideology of "social action." For the present, however, the potential of such a strategy was not great:

It should be emphasized that the possibilities of a real movement growing on the campus at this time are not great. . . . Perhaps the main stumbling block is the political atmosphere in the U.S. . . . There is, indeed, no viable movement in any section of society for social change. The labor unions are bureaucratized and inactive, if not corrupt. The organized liberals have compromised themselves on too many issues and are committed to working within the "Establishment" to such a degree that they do not form a real alternative or protest against it. The only forces capable of fostering any movement of social protest are the scattered socialists and pacifists and the few others who comprise the "radical" community. And against the entrenched forces of the "power elite" these few can have little effect. . . . However, the hope remains that something can happen. . . . Now, with the resurgence of concern on the campus, is the time to consider seriously some of the problems and possibilities for student political and social action.[25]

The Student Peace Union was not to be the organization that would "consider seriously some of the problems and possibilities for student political and social action." It was no accident that this analysis did not see the civil-rights struggle as a possible source of a movement for social change, and it reflects the character of the SPU as an extension of an older left not yet come to grips with the America of 1960. The fundamental pessimism about the prospects for a student movement, and the ties to YPSL, prevented such an examination. For, despite the different "types" of YPSLs in the SPU, the fundamental effect of YPSL on the ideological and organizational development of the SPU was to frame the issues and discussions in the terms of an earlier era. To the left of the fifties, capitalism seemed to have successfully—at least for the moment—muted the sources of domestic discontent, and only in the area of foreign policy could the left still offer a coherent critique that might find a receptive audience. The southern sit-ins had reached massive proportions in 1960 and 1961, and yet, in November of that year, the YPSL and the SPU could only debate whether or not a "peace movement" existed. While the sit-ins were recognized as having stirred a political awakening among students, to the YPSL and SPU leaders what was necessary was that this new energy be channeled into the "larger" issues of foreign policy.

This Old Left perspective also led the SPU to adopt a wary and often hostile attitude toward other groups on the student left. An ironic consequence of this attitude was that when the Students for a Democratic Society proposed a close working relationship with the SPU to build a "socialist" student movement,[26] the SPU leaders rejected the overture because they viewed the attempt as impossible and the SDS as too liberal. The national secretary of the SDS was a member of the SPU National Council in 1961, and a year earlier the leaders of the two organizations had exchanged membership cards, but by 1963 the SDS was emerging as the umbrella organization of a multi-issue student left, while the single-issue SPU was entering its death throes.[27]

The foreign policy focus of the SPU was both its strength and its weakness. The deep anxieties that are always caused by international crises outside the control of ordinary men and women had made possible the dramatic rise of the Student Peace Union. At its peak the SPU reached thousands of American students with a radical analysis of the cold war and its implications that they might otherwise never have heard. This same foreign policy focus, however, made the SPU vulnerable to sudden changes in the international situation over which it had no control. With the emerging detente between the Soviet Union and the United States that began in 1963, the days of the SPU were numbered, and its decline followed rapidly. Many of the lessons of the SPU experience would be lost on the later antiwar movement in the late sixties, and therein lies the real tragedy of the Student Peace Union.

For, in the final analysis, the SPU marked a transition in the American left. In its ties to YPSL and its focus on foreign policy, the SPU was a remnant of an earlier left. Its national leadership never was tempted by New Frontier liberalism and held the view that only socialism could provide meaningful change, but its practices were anti-Communist and exclusionary. Its leadership shared with the left of the fifties a deep pessimism about the possibilities of building a radical movement with broad appeal.

Alongside of these features that tied the SPU to the Old Left were other features that portended something new. The SPU was an *independent* student organization not accountable to any adult organization for its policies and programs. It was also an *action* organization whose members, for the most part, were far less interested in discussing the history and theory of radical social change than they were in acting to change society. Centralized leadership was avoided in the SPU, and local chapters developed their programs autonomously. Perhaps most important of all, the SPU provided a set of political experiences for thousands of members of a young generation that had grown up with little contact with political activity, and opened the door to new identities as "political beings."

The SPU died, and all too many of the lessons it provided had to be relearned by a later New Left. Its ties to the Old Left distorted and aborted its development, and even though many of the students who became active in politics through the SPU went on to participate in the New Left organizations that followed, any continuity of political development between the SPU and these later organizations was inhibited by the final decision of the leaders: to dissolve the SPU without urging the members to carry their experience into the growing SDS.[28] Fewer of the lessons might then have been lost, and as one of the SPU leaders observed in retrospect: "We should have given them the membership—we should have gone into [SDS] and been their foreign policy section in some sort of independent way. And we would have given them much strength.[29]"

Part II
A Democracy of Individual Participation

Some would have us believe that Americans feel contentment amidst prosperity—but might it not better be called a glaze above deeply-felt anxieties about their role in the new world? And if these anxieties produce a developed indifference to human affairs, do they not as well produce a yearning to believe there is an alternative to the present, that something can be done to change circumstances in the school, the workplaces, the bureaucracies, the government? It is to this latter yearning, at once the spark and engine of change, that we direct our present appeal. The search for truly democratic alternatives to the present, and a commitment to social experimentation with them, is a worthy and fulfilling human enterprise, one which moves us and, we hope, others today.

(Port Huron Statement)

Part II
A Democracy of Individuals and
Participation

4 On Theory

To most Americans, the New Left and the Students for a Democratic Society were one and the same. In the late sixties, it seemed that the SDS was involved in every activity associated with the New Left, and individuals like Tom Hayden and Rennie Davis became familiar to millions of TV viewers as spokesmen for whatever demonstration was going on at that moment. Such an identification greatly oversimplifies the complex and often varied development of a New Left during the last decade, but it does reflect the fact that somehow the development of the Students for a Democratic Society contained most of the ingredients that we associate with that New Left.

On the face of it, this is surprising, since one of the chief characteristics of the New Left supposedly was its independence from an older left. The SDS, unlike the Student Peace Union before it, was for many years the student department of the League for Industrial Democracy, a part of the "social-democratic" left with an organizational continuity reaching back to 1905.[1] And yet, somehow the SDS avoided the experience of the SPU and was able to become the "vanguard" of an emerging New Left. By examining the process by which the SDS became truly independent of its ties to the LID, we may gain some greater insight into just what was "new" about the New Left.

It has been claimed that the New Left, in addition to being organizationally independent of the Old Left, differed from earlier movements aiming at radical social change both in its ideology and its practice. Massimo Teodori has suggested that these differences included the New Left's emphasis on "de-centralization" and multiplicity of structures, "participatory democracy" at all levels, the abolition of institutionalized bureaucracies, and the "non-exclusion" of political viewpoints differing from those of the New Left.[2] Kirkpatrick Sale has written an exhaustive history of the organizational development of SDS which documents these characteristics,[3] but in this chapter (and in the one that follows) I will examine how and why these characteristics were combined to provide a basis for the theory and practice of SDS. My purpose in this examination is not to provide a history of SDS (Sale has devoted 657 pages to that task), but rather to outline those factors that shaped the conscious (and self-conscious) efforts of the SDS activists to forge a New Left.

Unlike the impersonal social forces that may generate discontent among social groups, the development of a theory and practice to explain that discontent and express it in some organized fashion is a subjective activity by men and women rooted in concrete historical settings. Their attempts to "understand" the sources of their discontent and to act on that understanding are reflections not of "things as they are," but of "things as they seem." To gain an understanding of the former, however, it is first necessary to understand *why* things are as they seem. In sociological terms, this means examining the various institutional and group settings—and the networks of interaction within these—in which such subjective perceptions develop. Only then can we seek broader explanations of the social forces that give rise to those settings and interactions. Only then can we explain the *praxis*—the unity of theory and practice—that this subjective activity represents.

Out of the Old

The experience of the Student League for Industrial Democracy was typical of the student left during the fifties. In the early fifties the group initiated a new educational campaign around such themes as "Planning in a Free Society" and "The Conflicting Ideologies of our Time," but the anti-Communist fervor of the McCarthy Era demanded a clear stand on the loyalty of political groups. In a "Statement on the World Situation," devoted primarily to foreign policy matters, the national executive committee of SLID made its stand clear in 1951:

If this trend continues, all liberal and socialist-minded men and women will be under fire in these coming days. It is up to all liberals to fight against unjust charges, and to force the authorities and the public to clearly differentiate between socialists and liberals, on the one hand, and on the other hand, communists whose primary loyalty is that to imperialistic Russia.[4]

Like the majority of the non-Communist Left, SLID joined the attack on the Communists in the hope of holding on to support from liberals and segments of labor. The attempt failed, however, and even with the able service of field secretaries such as James Farmer (later national chairman of CORE) and Gabriel Kolko during the early fifties, those years were dismal ones in which a handful of members in a few chapters sponsored occasional lectures and debates.

There was little resemblance between the SLID that had helped mobilize 150,000 students in a national strike during 1935, and the SLID of 1957. Although it maintained a student secretary (whose salary was paid by the adult LID), the budget was so diminished that organizing trips were infrequent, and elected officers devoted little time to the organization. The general attitude toward SLID on the campuses was reflected in a letter from a Harvard member:

As a radical group it inspires only disinterest, and nothing is deadlier than apathy, since it appears rapidly to effect the members also. As an educational organization it simply cannot stand the competition.[5]

The stagnation and decline SLID experienced was not, of course, primarily a result of internal weakness, but reflected the general avoidance of political activity that characterized college students at the time. The center of political debate had shifted to the right, and SLID was caught up in the general reaction. The impact of this reaction was not only manifest in the failure to organize on campus, but also in the political stance of the leadership. Responding to a local chapter's threat to withdraw from the organization, the SLID field secretary agreed that socialism was no longer on the agenda:

We have not, since the second world war, been socialist in ideology, tho there have been many active socialists in the organization—socialists who are now becoming smaller in the leadership and more defensive intellectually. But I agree that the socialist connection should be minimized—I used to consider myself a socialist, but no longer do, since the word is now meaningless. But most of the members are not socialist. The Yale group has a significant Republican group, and Yale and Wisconsin are the two largest chapters. And in certain respects we are less radical than the Americans for Democratic Action.[6]

The 1957 convention of SLID drew only thirty-nine delegates, but those same delegates managed to pass some sixty resolutions on foreign and domestic policy.[7] The ironies of political life in the fifties were often evident in these resolutions, as when the delegates, after declaring it SLID policy, "To begin our second half-century by making as fundamental a break with all outworn conventions of political thought as that which our forebears had the conviction and intellectual integrity to begin the first," went on to immediately reiterate, "We shall continue to refuse to cooperate with any groups whose aims or methods contradict such a commitment to democracy."[8]

Apparently, the "outworn conventions of political thought" did not include overt anticommunism, even when the need for unity among the dwindling left was obvious. Indeed, the same passage continued,

In these days of shifting party lines, it is important to note that a policy of "anti-Stalinism" is meaningless. Stalinists, as well as Leninists, Bolsheviks, Fascists, Falangists, Trotskyists and other exponents or apologists for anti-democratic goals and methods, are now "anti-Stalinist."[9]

In commenting on the continued anticommunism, one staff member who attended the convention later observed:

We felt we would be betraying those who had opposed Stalin's dictatorship from the left if we collaborated here, or abroad, with those who defended it. Obviously, the overwhelming propaganda of the time twisted all this to completely underplay the degree to which the West was also at fault and the ways in which our own attitudes would be used by the CIA or others.[10]

The decline of SLID continued the following year, with the 1958 convention attracting thirteen delegates (only four of whom had not been at the previous convention).[11] Toward the end of that year, however, a gradual change in the character of the organization began to take place, a transition that was to culminate with the Port Huron convention of 1962. In organizational terms, this was really a transition from the Old Left to the New Left, and it involved a hard-fought struggle between those whose issues were framed in terms of a view of the "working class" as the only source of progressive change, and those whose issues were framed in terms of a new set of discontents that had been generated during the cold war years.

In personalized terms, the start of this transition could be traced back to one of those unnoticed historical moments a year earlier (1957), when a young student at the University of Michigan in Ann Arbor joined the newly formed Political Issues Club. The son of a college professor who had been a member of the LID, Robert Allan (Al) Haber was one of those students who, without any great knowledge of the Old Left, was developing an interest in political action as a means of social change. A few years later, out of the nucleus formed in the Political Issues Club, the VOICE student political party would become an important base for building the New Left, but in 1957 and 1958, such political activity was still a lonely business. When his name was suggested by local SLID contacts as a possible candidate for the National Executive Committee, Haber wrote to the national office about his view of political work:

My enthusiasm is still at a high pitch and I'm doing my best to avoid that disillusionment which seems to be almost a necessary concommitant of trying to get anyone to think about anything, to say nothing of getting them to act. . . .

There is though always the perennial question of "so what?," "what good is it going to do?" I think that fundamentally this is the question facing the PIC, and perhaps it is the question facing SLID. PIC was ineffective because we worried about it. . . .

You have to take it as an article of faith that getting people to think is worthwhile in itself and that wherever you are is the best place to start and now is the best time. You hope that if enough people are made aware of contemporary problems and the values at stake, their force will somehow be felt.[12]

The almost existential "leap of faith" Haber described was to become a common denominator of the New Left emphasis on *action*, and his concern for the "values at stake" would provide the starting point for the New Left's attempt to develop a distinct political identity. The shift away from SLID's role as an educational effort of the social democratic left engaged in a "holding" operation towards the SDS role as an organizational "center" for the activist student left began with the election of Haber as vice-president of SLID in 1959. In 1960 he was appointed as field secretary, and with his election as president later the same year, the stage was set for a major internal struggle over the future direction of the organization.

This changing direction was reflected in the SLID magazine, *Venture*, which began publishing in April of 1959. The first three issues of the magazine carried articles on unemployment, the Soviet Union, socialism in England, union apathy, South Africa, the Vienna Youth Festival, and Polish socialism.[13] There were also articles on "alienation," liberalism, utopianism, pacifism, and anticommunism (viewed favorably). In the spring of 1960, *Venture* carried articles on Polish socialism, anti-Semitism, and the civil-rights movement. The September (1960) issue reported on the White House Conference on Children and Youth, an NSA conference on the sit-in movement, the civil-rights movement, and an SDS conference on "Human Rights in the North." These last two issues also discussed the growth of a student movement, the tactic of sit-ins, and the distinction between protest and radicalism.

Thus, within a one-year period, the focus of *Venture* shifted away from a despairing view of the domestic scene and an almost exclusive emphasis on foreign policy, to a hopeful view of the civil-rights movement as a *potential* base for a new student movement. The articles stressed, however, the need for a *multi-issue* approach to building such a student movement. The magazine also concentrated less, as time went on, on analyzing the structure of society, and more on developing strategies for change.[14] These changes in the content of *Venture* reflected the changing programmatic focus of the organization under Haber's leadership.

As part of this change in image, SLID changed its name, in 1960, to Students for a Democratic Society, largely because the term "industrial democracy" had fallen out of use and was unfamiliar to most students. The direction in which Haber was pushing the organization became clearer in the spring of that year, when the SDS sponsored a conference on "Human Rights in the North" at the University of Michigan. Haber was one of the two directors of the conference, which, unlike previous SLID conferences, sought to develop a program of action rather than simply to provide an "education" experience.[15] Instead of speakers from the academic community, the conference brought leaders of SNCC and CORE together with white students from the North to discuss support for the southern students. Several recommendations emerged from the conference, including a call for the publication of a national student newsletter on civil rights and the convocation of a national student conference on civil rights the following fall. It called upon SDS to "take the initiative in calling a meeting of civil rights organizations for the purpose of planning the fall national students conference and putting out a newsletter," and it urged each delegate to organize a "broadly based *interracial* civil rights action group on his campus." Finally, the conference closed with an appeal: "All legitimate means of action and influence must be used to make civil rights the central domestic issue in American politics."[16]

Following this conference, Haber was hired as field secretary of SDS and immediately began planning for the annual convention to be held on June 17. Following up on the visible connection with civil rights that the May conference had given SDS, the theme of the convention was "Student Radicalism—1960," and it attracted seventy students from fifteen colleges.[17] Instead of passing volumes of resolutions, the convention delegates devoted themselves to debating the fundamental orientation of the organization. One major discussion centered around the distinction between liberalism and radicalism, and there was considerable disagreement over whether political action was justified by moral considerations alone, or whether a kind of "lesser evil" theory should guide any decision to engage in protest activities.[18]

It was at this convention that Haber was elected president, and not long thereafter that the split between the "old guard" and the newer radicals broke into the open. With his elected and appointed positions, Haber was in a position to push for complete reorientation of the SDS, but his effort met considerable resistance. In a report to the LID board of directors, in October of 1960, he reported that the SDS had six functioning chapters, five more in active formation, and another five in early stages of formation.[19] He proposed a major effort to implement the recommendations of the Human Rights in the North Conference, to organize chapters in the South, and to establish close working relations with civil-rights, peace, and student groups. This touched off a major struggle which first broke out at the LID Student Activities Committee meeting in December.[20] Haber argued that the SDS was "out of phase with what is going on on campus," and that it should become a "national center for liberal activity providing background in areas such as civil rights." He was opposed by two of the "old guard" student members (who were also members of the YPSL "realignment" tendency), who argued:

We are an educational organization, not a protest group. . . . We don't want to be affiliated with civil rights or civil liberties groups as such—they must not be civil rights chapters, but simply chapters.[21]

At a meeting of the SDS National Executive Committee the following month, Haber was supported by only one other member and was forced temporarily to retreat.[22] Instead, he used the administrative machinery to isolate those who opposed him within the organization, and began building a new network outside the formal structure of the organization. By May of 1961, most of the "old guard" had withdrawn from active participation, and Haber could report that membership had risen from 250 in the fall to 450 in May, and that the organization had nine chapters. Six were active: Chicago, Michigan, Yale, Brooklyn, Harvard and Western Reserve. Not functioning were Columbia, N.Y. City At-Large, and Syracuse—all of which had been YPSL and "old guard" strongholds.[23] At the same time, he reported that no people were willing to do office work, that *Venture* had not been issued since September, that no mailings had gone out to the membership, that the internal bulletin had not been issued, and that "we must, in a phrase, start from scratch."[24]

Toward a New Left

With the withdrawal and isolation of the Old Left within SDS, the possibility of a new political direction for the organization increased. Before this potential could be developed, however, there remained the problem of relations between the adult LID and the SDS. As the "old guard" (often, YPSL) students withdrew, they lodged sharp protests with the parent organization, and throughout the spring of 1961, the future of the organization hung in the balance. Haber argued that under his leadership the membership had doubled, and that he had succeeded in developing a cadre of leaders interested in building the organization, but that in order to continue this process the LID must support a strong national office structure with a comprehensive program.[25] The LID leaders initially rejected this approach, instead ordering a continued focus on education and a decentralized structure, and at the end of March, Haber offered his resignation.[26]

He was bargaining from strength, however, for he had built up a network of people who were prepared to create a new organization if the LID was unwilling to provide a home. The LID elders asked Haber to withhold his resignation and to propose a new program for the SDS, and on May 4 he responded:

Personnel: I have eight people committed to work for the organization.
Finances: I propose to raise the money necessary to carry out the program.
Program: I propose to make the SDS the intellectual and program focus of liberal, radical, and democratic activity on the campus.[27]

In a thinly veiled threat, he added (in still another letter) that he would attempt to form a new organization if the LID rejected his proposals:

There are a group of eight people who are anxious to begin. I have been faced with the decision of whether I try to postpone activity until the LID solidified its own position. . . . As of now, I am beginning in earnest the activity of developing a new organization. . . . We will solicit money and adult support, we will attempt to hold a convention. It should be clear that this course will involve the solicitation for money and support of many friends of the LID.[28]

In spelling out his program proposals, Haber argued that the SDS should take a flexible attitude toward membership and chapter relationships, and that the national office should serve as a clearing house for publication, research, and information about the left, as well as a channel for such material to campus groups. The SDS would serve as a liaison between adult and campus groups and would attempt to encourage students to continue political activity after graduation. He argued that, while the SDS should not be an "action" organization, it should encourage direct action at the same time that it pointed out the limitations of action and the need for an understanding of the "root" problems. On the crucial (to the LID) issue of anticommunism and the need to "exclude" those who sympathized with "Stalinism," Haber argued that Communist influence on students was almost nil, and suggested

that we be willing on an individual basis to involve the "stalinoid" type . . . that our line in opposition to communism and totalitarianism is unequivocal, but it is expressed primarily in terms of a positive commitment to democratic values, that we have some finesse in raising questions of political integrity and avoid "redbaiting."[29]

On May 24, 1961, the LID accepted a compromise offered by Haber that instructed the SDS to call a conference in September which would bring together under the SDS banner "the leaders of campus groups on the democratic left"—the purpose of which was to recruit new members into SDS.[30] Haber was appointed conference administrator, and the LID ordered the postponement of the 1961 convention until 1962 to allow the new members time to learn about the organization.

The conference was held on a farm near New York City from September 8 to 10 and focused on the theme "The Ideologies, Politics, and Controversies of the Student Movement." Those attending approved Haber's position on the future direction of SDS and decided to function as a northern liaison for SNCC, to establish an organizing program for southern campuses, and to initiate student-faculty research seminars on problems of "peace." Tom Hayden, a former editor of the *Michigan Daily,* was selected as field organizer for the southern project.[31]

The conference also chose an interim steering committee to function until the next convention, and the new direction was evident in the choices. Haber was elected president, Bob Ross (the only member of the old NEC who had supported Haber) as vice-president. Among the other members were Paul Booth and Rebecca Adams (who had organized an independent peace research and action group at Swarthmore), Sandra Cason Hayden (Tom's wife, and a SNCC worker), Tim Jenkins (a founder of SNCC, and black vice-president of NSA), James Monsonis of SNCC, and Bob Zellner of CORE.[32] To this group fell the task of making SDS the "national center" envisioned by Haber.

Thus, before the summer of 1962, the SDS had divorced itself, in fact, from its Old Left ties. The civil-rights movement replaced the labor movement as the central source of radical social change in the eyes of the new members. To Haber and the new members he recruited, anticommunism was a tired and stale issue not worthy of serious debate or concern, and in their view anyone involved in action for change should be welcomed in the SDS ranks. In the months following the September conference, the organization moved to deepen its ties with the civil-rights movement, and to consolidate under its organizational apparatus the diverse local groups concerned with peace and civil liberties. While Tom Hayden travelled the South on behalf of SDS, creating a visible presence in the southern movement and reporting back in long letters that were distributed to the membership, Haber concentrated on building local chapters. The strong Swarthmore Political Action Committee and the FDR Four Freedoms Club (New York) became tied to SDS, and the organization joined with the Progressive Student League at Oberlin to sponsor a conference on campus political parties. Throughout the winter and spring, most of the energy went into planning the June convention—where the birth of a New Left was to be announced.[33]

Port Huron

Although the SDS, under Haber's leadership, had won a measure of independence for a course of action that was very different from the practice of the Old Left, it had yet to systematically and coherently articulate the political positions this practice implied. At a meeting of the interim steering committee in December of 1961, it had been decided that the June convention should concentrate on adopting a long "organizational statement of values, social analysis, and broad guidelines of policy," tentatively called the "SDS Manifesto."[34] Tom Hayden was assigned the task of preparing an initial draft, which the convention would revise. Through the winter and spring, Hayden circulated memos describing his progress and soliciting input on the issues, and some chapters and members responded.

When the convention was finally held in June, fifty-nine participants showed up. Although many states were represented, the greatest number were from New York and Michigan.[35] Representatives from the Young Democrats and SNCC were seated as delegates, while representatives from the National Student Christian Federation, Young Christian Students, and Progressive Youth Organizing Committee were seated as observers.[36]

The discussions were long and sometimes heated, and the process of the meeting left a lasting impression on the participants:

The people were mostly student activists, leader types. . . . There were a number of people who were active in NSA and student government . . . there were people with certain Old Left backgrounds . . . there were a sprinkling of SNCC people . . . and older social democrats. It was a very intense thing . . . there was a tremendous amount of small group discussions that were very lengthy. . . . Then there were these endless plenary sessions that would go on from ten in the morning until five at night.[37]

Out of these discussions, however, there emerged a consensus that was based on the common sentiments of this diverse group:

The thing we all felt—the people that were at Port Huron on the whole were activists—it wasn't simply that they were intellectuals, they were activists in other movements. The thing that there was sort of agreement on was the need to transcend each of these movements, that the movements were going to be dead unless they could articulate a broader strategy. If the civil-rights movement just relied on nonviolent direct action, then it would not go anywhere. It needed political strategy, it needed to relate to economic issues. If the peace movement just relied on vigils and demonstrations, it wouldn't get anywhere unless it saw the links between the peace issue and the civil-rights movement.[38]

After much discussion and revision, the basic thrust of the draft documents was accepted, and a styles committee was selected to redraft the document and prepare a version for public circulation. Soon to be known as the *Port Huron Statement,* the document was prefaced by a note proclaiming the provisional nature of the analysis: "It is presented as a document with which SDS officially identifies, but also as a living document open to change with our times and experiences."[39]

The *Port Huron Statement* (PHS) attempted to provide a broad framework that both catalogued the reasons why basic social change was needed in American society and that suggested a strategy for bringing such change about. At the outset, it asserted the special characteristics of those who prepared it: "We are people of this generation, bred in at least modest comfort, housed now in universities, looking uncomfortably to the world we inherit."[40]

The message was one both of disillusionment and hope and reflected the same existential commitment that seemed to be at the heart of the new radicalism:

We began to sense that what we had originally seen as the American Golden Age
was actually the decline of an era. . . .

Our work is guided by the sense that we may be the last generation in the experiment
with living. But we are a minority—the vast majority of our people regard the
temporary equilibriums of our society and world as externally functional
parts. . . . Beneath the reassuring tones of the politicians, beneath the common
opinion that America will "muddle through" . . . is the pervading feeling that there
simply are no alternatives, that our times have witnessed the exhaustion not only of
Utopias, but of any new departures as well. . . .

Some would have us believe that Americans feel contentment amidst prosperity
—but might it not be better called a glaze above deeply-felt anxieties about their role
in the new world? And if these anxieties produce a developed indifference to human
affairs, do they not as well produce a yearning to believe there *is* an alternative to
the present, that something *can* be done to change circumstances. . . . It is to this
latter yearning . . . that we direct our present appeal.[41]

To the young SDS radicals, the source of these anxieties—as well as the
yearning for alternatives—were rooted in a distortion of human values.
They began their appeal with a statement of their values:

We regard *men* as infinitely precious and possessed of unfulfilled capacities for
reason, freedom, and love. . . . We oppose the depersonalization that reduces
human beings to the status of things. . . . Men have unrealized potential for
self-cultivation, self-direction, self-understanding, and creativity. . . .

Human relationships should involve fraternity and honesty. . . . Personal links
between man and man are needed, especially to go beyond the partial and fragmen-
tary bonds of function. . . .

As the individualism we affirm is not egoism, the selflessness we affirm is not
self-elimination. . . . We believe in generosity of a kind that imprints one's unique
individual qualities in the relation to other men. . . .

That work should involve incentives worthier than money or survival. It should be
educative, not stultifying; creative, not mechanical; self-directed, not manipulated,
encouraging independence . . . a sense of dignity and a willingness to accept social
responsibility.[42]

The most important value, however, was something they called "participatory democracy":

That decision making of basic social consequence be carried on by public groupings;

—that politics be seen positively as the art of collectively creating an acceptable
pattern of social relations;

—that politics has the function of bringing people out of isolation and into community, thus being a necessary, though not sufficient, means of finding meaning in
personal life;

—that the political order should serve to clarify problems in a way instrumental to
their solution; it should provide outlets for the expression of personal grievance and
aspiration; opposing views should be organized so as to illuminate choices and

facilitate the attainment of goals; channels should be commonly available to relate men to knowledge and power so that private problems . . . are formulated as general issues.[43]

The document distinguished between the present subjective apathy of students caused by their powerlessness in the face of momentous events, and the objective conditions of American society that encouraged that apathy. Its critique of the economy was rather simplistic, however, focusing on the "remote control economy" and the "military industrial complex." With respect to the labor movement as a source of change, it saw little hope:

In some measure, labor has succumbed to institutionalization, its social idealism waning under the tendencies of bureaucracy, materialism, business ethics . . . not only is this true of the labor elites, but as well of some of the rank-and-file. Many of the latter are indifferent unionists, uninterested in meetings, alienated from the complexities of the labor management negotiating apparatus, lulled to comfort by the accessibility of luxury and the opportunity of long-term contracts.[44]

With respect to foreign policy, the document charged that militarism and anticommunism were the main cornerstones of US policy, and it argued strongly that this anticommunism was a "paranoia" that must be ended if rational change was to occur:

It would seem reasonable to expect that in America the basic issues of the Cold War should be rationally and fully debated, between persons of every opinion. . . . It would seem, too, that there should be a way for a person or an organization to oppose communism *without* contributing to the common fear of associations and public actions. But these things do not happen; instead there is finger-pointing and comical debate about the most serious of issues. This trend of events on the domestic scene, towards greater irrationality on major questions, moves us to greater concern than does the "international threat" of domestic communism.[45]

After continuing the indictment with a detailed discussion of the racist character of American society and politics, the document at last turned to proposing solutions for the problems it described. It called for phased disarmament, for the building up of machinery for conflict resolution through international action, and for a long-term effort to industrialize the "third world" on its own terms. Domestically, it called for a realignment of the two-party system along liberal-conservative lines, for the creation of "mechanisms of voluntary association" for political action, and for making corporations publicly responsible to social needs rather than private profit.

Finally, the document turned from its analysis of the present situation to a discussion of possible strategies for change. It saw hope for a new movement for social change in a broadened civil-rights movement, but it saw the peace movement as having only the limited potential of building local bases for multi-issue organizing—and it stressed the need (however difficult this might prove in practice) to reach out to segments of organized labor. Despite these few hopeful signs, the writers concluded that the power and vision necessary to build the kind of movement they envisioned was not likely to come from any of these sources. Instead, they looked to the university as the place where such a "New Left" might be formed:

Any new left in America must be . . . a left with real intellectual skills, committed to deliberativeness, honesty, reflection as working tools. The university permits the political life to be adjunct to the academic one. . . .

A new left must be distributed in significant social roles throughout the country. The universities are distributed in such a manner.

A new left must consist of younger people who matured in the post-war world, and partially be directed to the recruitment of younger people. The university is an obvious beginning point.

A new left must include liberals and socialists, the former for their relevance, the latter for their sense of thoroughgoing reforms in the system. The university is a more sensible place than a political party for these two traditions to begin to discuss their differences and look for political synthesis.

A new left must start controversy across the land, if national policies and national apathy are to be reversed. The ideal university is a community of controversy. . . .

A new left must transform modern complexity into issues that can be understood and felt close up by every human being. It must give form to the feelings of helplessness and indifference, so that people may see the political, social and economic sources of their private troubles and organize to change society.[46]

This, then, was to be the strategy that guided SDS in its first years. Beginning with the university, they would attempt to build a student movement that could link up with others struggling to change society, and in the process of building that movement break through the subjective apathy that prevented men from discerning the possibility of overcoming their objective oppression. To implement this strategy, the convention chose a new National Executive Committee and elected Tom Hayden as president, Paul Booth as vice-president, Jim Monsonis as national secretary, and Steve Max as field director.[47]

In the process leading up to Port Huron, and in the actual writing of the *PHS*, the "elite" of a New Left was formed, and the internal development of SDS during the next several years was largely a reflection of the experiences of that elite. The formative years of SDS, and the Port Huron convention itself, provided a commonly shared set of experiences for this nucleus of students during which they attempted to develop a common set of definitions of their experience. The *Port Huron Statement* was that set of definitions—an articulation of values, a partial vision of a desirable future, and the beginning of a program to realize those values and that future. Because it did not root those values, that vision, and that program in an historical analysis of their genesis, however, the document was also a *personal* statement of the drafters. That it was not uniquely an expression of their personal experiences, alone, was evident in the popularity of the *PHS* achieved in the years following; C. Clark Kissinger claims that from its writing in 1962, until its first publication in 1964, 20,000 copies of the *PHS* were distributed in mimeographed form.[48] But it offered no explanation of why those values had become central to this generation of students. What this meant in the years after Port Huron was that the interpretation of those values, and the development of strategies for implementing them, took the form of a debate within the original "elite" based upon their individual experiences, and without consideration of the historical process in which it was embedded. Moreover, it took place as a reflection upon the experiences of this elite without reference to the experiences of those who would follow their lead.

Just how radical a departure from the analysis and traditions of the Old Left the *Port Huron Statement* was became clear even before the styles committee had time to rework the draft. Haber, Hayden, Ross, and Max were summoned to a meeting of the LID Student Activities Committee on June 28 and were confronted with a bitter attack on the analysis in the draft document as being soft on communism and overly hostile to the United States, as well as criticism of the convention for being nonrepresentative and for seating the PYOC observer.[49] On July 3, Haber and Hayden went to Washington on SDS business, and while they were away the LID Executive Committee (of which Haber was a member) met in secret to repudiate the document—which they had not seen in revised form—and to suspend the SDS. Haber and Hayden were directed to appear at a hearing on July 6,

to discover whether or not the officers of the SDS acted and plan to act in accordance with the basic principles of the parent organization. . . . Until that time no materials, manifestoes, constitutions, or any publications having to do with policy in any way, shape, or form whatsoever may be mailed or distributed by the students under the identification of the SDS.[50]

Haber and Hayden responded by protesting the lack of due process and by calling the SDS National Executive Committee to New York to assist them. At the hearing on July 6, the LID fired the entire SDS staff and put the office under supervision (including new locks on the doors), while the NEC voted to support Haber and Hayden and to appeal the decision.[51] The dispute continued throughout the summer, and while the LID finally agreed to allow the revised manifesto to be issued and to reinstate the staff with the kind of autonomy it had demanded, as far as the students were concerned, the continued relationship was little more than a formality that assisted fund raising.[52]

Thus, even before the full implications of the politics put forth in the

PHS could be explored in practice, the new activists were forced, once again, to defend their views and define their relationship to a part of the Old Left. Tom Hayden may have been summarizing the feelings of all of them when he remarked, at the end of the meeting with the LID committee, that he felt as though, "I'm dealing with a cold war situation in this room."[53] The hostility and misunderstanding that ensued were not merely a result of differences over certain agreed upon issues (as had been the case in the internecine warfare of the Old Left), but reflected a basic disagreement over what the issues were. To those in the non-Communist Old Left, the key issues were the "betrayal" of human decency and democratic principles by the Communists both in Russia and here at home, and the need to maintain a base in the liberal and labor constituencies which might bring moderate reforms. For the new activists centered in the SDS of 1962, the central issues were the failure of New Deal reforms to eliminate racism, poverty, and militarism as central features of American life. It was not manipulation by some domestic agents of foreign, totalitarian communism that threatened democratic values, but rather the complacent affluence of cold war liberals.

In attempting to present a *theoretical* statement of these differences, however, the SDS activists were led to a different interpretive paradigm than the Old Left. The Old Left paradigm viewed social inequality as an inevitable outcome of the exploitation of human labor inherent in the capitalist mode of production, and the "industrial proletariat" as the principal agency for change—both because it is the main victim of this exploitation, and because of its size and centrality in the capitalist system. In terms of strategies for change, the Communist left called for a "vanguard" party following the principles of Marxism-Leninism to lead the working class in the overthrow of capitalism, while the social-democratic left called for an alliance between organized labor, minority groups, and liberals to wage a peaceful struggle for the gradual adoption of socialist programs. For both segments of the Old Left, the source of inequality, as well as the source of change, was rooted in the class conflict generated by industrial capitalism.

This Old Left paradigm confronted the new activists not only as a *theory* of the sources of inequality and change, but also as a *practice* that had failed. To these students, the Old Left was a discredited left which had failed to establish any significant social base. The Communist left was discredited by its identification with the totalitarian policies of the Soviet Union, while the social-democratic left was discredited by its support for the cold war policies of the United States. The basic paradigm of the Old Left, moreover, was discredited by the apparent lack of "class consciousness" in the industrial proletariat, and by the apparent "stabilization" of American capitalism.

The response of the new activists was to tentatively put forth a paradigm that saw the source of social inequality in the uneven access to *power* engendered by large-scale organization. The "iron law of oligarchy" was seen as a greater source of inequality than "class conflict," and the potential for change, therefore, lay in the decentralization of power and in the organization of the powerless. In the paradigm of the New Left, "democracy" replaced "socialism" as the defining characteristic of the egalitarian society, and in the early practice of the New Left, decentralization, voluntarism, and nonexclusionism were consciously substituted for the centralization, discipline, and exclusion that characterized the organizational practice of much of the Old Left.

In its early development, then, the response of the New Left to the paradigm of the Old Left took the form of a revolt against Marxism in which, as Horowitz has noted, the radical notion of the *mass* was substituted for the socialist notion of *class*.[54] By emphasizing their common powerlessness, the New Left could stress the potential unity of this "mass," rather than its present fragmentation along racial and class lines. By rooting inequality in the characteristics of bureaucratic organization, moreover, the New Left paradigm fostered an emphasis on spontaneity and *will* over and against organization as the method of struggle.

The Rejection of Liberal Solutions

In the year following the Port Huron convention, the SDS leaders deepened their political analysis. The *PHS* had spoken hopefully of the desire for change and had indicted American policy in both foreign and domestic spheres, but it had not found an analysis that could show how, and from what sources, change might come. Although it saw the civil-rights and peace movements as hopeful signs, it argued that these could not provide the basis for a long-term movement for change, and ended up emphasizing the university as a place to begin. Politically, the statement did not go beyond "realignment" as the short-term goal of radical activity.

As the SDS deepened its ties to the civil-rights movement during 1963, and as the detente in the cold war emerged, the leaders began to develop a sharper analysis of how chance might come. At the 1963 convention, a new statement, *America and the New Era*, was adopted, and the analysis went considerably beyond that in *PHS*.[55] After arguing that the cold war was breaking down due to several factors—the reemergence of Europe as an economic entity; the emergence of the third world as a source of revolutionary upsurge; the disruption of nuclear weapons as a result of their proliferation—the document went on to foresee increasingly frequent domestic crises resulting from the economic consequences of automation and the continuing existence of racial inequality. More important, the drafters argued that the New Frontier programs failed to offer any solution to these crises, offering instead only increased manipulation of social life and tokenism. In a significant shift from the *PHS*, the new document proposed a strategy of radical activity *within* existing "insurgent" movements, rather than solely at the university:

Such tasks can best be accomplished through work by activists *where they are*. The primary strategic goal of the movement . . . is the development of *locally autonomous* insurgent political organization and action.[56]

Although the final version of the statement was less forceful than the draft[57] on the matter of working off campus, it did emphasize that "efforts at creating insurgent politics could be the organization of constituencies expressing, for the first time in this generation, the needs of ordinary men for a decent life."[58] Thus, even though the attempt to build a New Left based on students had barely begun, the leadership of SDS was moving away from a view of students as the vanguard in search of a broader base for political opposition. *America and the New Era* offers a view of a New Left in which students play a key role because of the skills they have developed, but not as a student movement oriented toward changing the university system.

While the *Port Huron Statement* was an attempt to spell out the *values* of a New Left that led to an oppositional stance, *America and the New Era* was an attempt to develop concrete strategies for change based on those values. Without any historical and economic analysis to explain those values and strategies, however, it was possible to treat them in isolated pieces and as of equal priority. What this led to was the creation of several different "projects" reflecting the interests of different members of the SDS elite, and to increasing competition between these projects (and the strategies they implied) for the limited resources of the organization.

By far the most important of these—and the largest—was the Economic Research and Action Project (ERAP). Conceived by Al Haber as a "labor project," the initial idea behind ERAP was to develop a means of stimulating discussion and analysis of economic issues within SDS and among students, and particularly of acquainting "middle-class" students with the facts of life about "working-class" existence.[59] SDS obtained a $5000 grant from the United Automobile Workers to initiate the project in August of 1963, but the analysis in *America and the New Era* led to an alteration in the original concept of the project.[60] The analysis in the *ANE* document seemed to require an emphasis on involving students in off-campus participation in various movements, rather than solely on the radical education of students. Haber was allotted half of the money to develop a handbook on economic issues and to publish an economic bulletin sympathetic, yet critical, of the activities of organized labor. The other half of the money went to fund Joe Chabot as a "community organizer" for SDS in Chicago, to organize unemployed white youth.[61]

This decision represented a compromise between those who saw SDS primarily as a student organization concerned with building a left-oriented student movement, and those who saw the organization as a "vanguard" for building a broad radical movement based on blacks, poor people, and students. Friction between these two conceptions increased during the fall, and at the December meeting of the National Council, they met head on. Two perspectives on the development of the organization were presented to the council, one by Al Haber, and the other by Tom Hayden. Haber argued that the American system was hardly ready to collapse, and that the task of SDS as a student organization with limited resources was to concentrate on campus organizing to build a student movement that would develop an analysis of the functioning of capitalism.[62] The primary focus was to be on research, and action projects would be developed only after research indicated what the dimensions of a radical program should be.

Hayden countered by arguing that the "new insurgencies" outlined in *America and the New Era* were a reality that reflected the breakdown of "mainstream institutions," and that the SDS should push such insurgent movements along a "revolutionary trajectory" by supporting short-term reformist demands, while at the same time developing indigenous radical political organizations that could prevent the movements from being co-opted. Thus, the focus of SDS should be on recruiting students to work in local communities. After heated discussion, the Hayden proposal was overwhelmingly adopted, and the National Council set community organizing as the main priority for work in the coming year.[63]

While the debate over ERAP was, in part, a debate about the proper constituency of SDS, it also reflected a disagreement within the elite about the stability of American institutions and the correct strategy for radical change. Although the elite had, from the outset, shared a desire not to be connected with the Old Left, their attitudes toward "Kennedy liberals" were more ambiguous and diverse. Most of the leaders of the organization thought of themselves as "socialists" of some sort, but they believed the best way to build a radical student movement was through the "radicalization" of liberal students. Moreover, they initially saw the differences between adult liberals and themselves as mainly one of *degree,* as their initial focus on "realignment" indicated.

Throughout 1962 and 1963, these attitudes changed as a result of their contact with adult liberals. In planning the February 1962 demonstration against nuclear testing, the SDS people had come in contact with adult liberal "peace types" centered in an organization called Turn Toward Peace, and found these liberals as offensive as the "Old Leftists" they scorned. As one SDS leader described his reaction: "I realized that there was a type of anticommunism which I found was as revolting as Soviet apologism . . . and essentially I saw them as either consciously or unconsciously siding with the United States in the cold war."[64]

Even more important was their contact with liberals in the Kennedy administration who shattered their faith that reasoned argument was all that was needed to obtain progressive changes in government policies. The Bay of Pigs invasion and the Cuban missile crisis provided the first storm warnings in their romance with the New Frontier, but the process of disillusionment was a gradual one which finally culminated with the refusal to seat the Mississippi Freedom Democratic party delegates at the Democratic convention, in 1964, and the escalation of the war in Vietnam, a year later. One former SDS leader recalled being horrified and appalled by his meeting with Adam Yarmolinsky, a special assistant to Secretary of Defense McNamara. The SDS people had gone to the meeting to discuss their concerns about civil defense policy, and they found that the assumptions on which Yarmolinsky based his position were, to them, suicidal and genocidal assumptions.[65] The Cuban missile crisis provided a similar shock, as the young activists' faith in reason was suddenly challenged by the realization that a "liberal" administration saw the Cuban revolution as so threatening to America that they were willing to start a nuclear war.

Liberalism, like the Old Left paradigm, became discredited in the eyes of the New Left. The birth, growth, and fragmentation of SDS overlapped almost exactly with eight years of "liberal Democrat" rule, and to a generation whose political awareness only extended back into the fifties, what the liberals did with their power in the sixties represented the full potential of liberalism as a social and political theory. Many of the early activists initially viewed their own activities on local campuses, in NSA, or even in SDS, as logical extensions of their "liberal" political views. The fervent rhetoric of John Kennedy seemed to embody the same vision of a politics of participation that they were developing, and programs like the "Peace Corps" offered a practical form for actualizing that vision. Tom Hayden, for example, was initially very enthusiastic about Kennedy. He introduced Kennedy to a student rally at the University of Michigan during the 1960 campaign and later consulted with administration officials on the plans for the Peace Corps. If anyone could bring humanistic and rational principles into the corridors of power, they felt, surely it would be Kennedy and the intellectuals around him.

Disillusionment set in quickly. Maybe Kennedy didn't know about the Bay of Pigs, but how could he threaten nuclear war over Cuba and Berlin? What possible rational justification could he invoke for the resumption of nuclear testing? Why did he not utilize the full powers of the federal government to protect and support the civil-rights movement? To these questions they could find no satisfactory answers that were sympathetic to

"New Frontier liberalism," and they became first sarcastic, and then hostile, toward those they had looked to for change. An SDS leaflet at the time of the Cuban missile crisis, for example, accused Kennedy of "playing a game of 'chicken' with mankind on the bumper."[66] The high-sounding call for a "war on poverty" by Kennedy's successor rang hollow after the sellout of the MFDP (led by archliberal Hubert Humphrey) at the 1964 convention, and with the escalation of the war in Vietnam, no shred of decency or rationality remained.

This gathering disillusionment required an explanation, but the only explanations that seemed to fit the facts grew increasingly harsh. The simple view that the liberals in power misunderstood the facts, but could be reasoned with, crumbled when the young people met the Yarmolinskys and Bundys. Not only did the liberal intellectuals share the cold war hysteria of their conservative counterparts, but they were openly willing to sacrifice progress for the poor and black to the raw dictates of political expediency. These liberal intellectuals were, in the words of one author, the "best and the brightest" of their generation—and yet, they offered only more of the same. Their real commitment, it seemed, was not to humanistic values, democratic principles, "peace," or "equality"—but only to power.

In the early years of development, the ambiguous attitude of the New Left toward liberalism was reflected in its conceptualization of the forces resisting change. The possibility that good men were being corrupted by power led to an emphasis on the "system" or the "power structure" as the locus of reaction. As the disenchantment grew, and explanations based on individual co-optation no longer sufficed, it became necessary to name that system and that power structure—and the name was "corporate liberalism." Carl Oglesby's speech to the November 1965 antiwar demonstration marked the culmination of disillusionment, and thereafter the anti-Communist liberals were viewed not simply as misguided, but as *responsible* for poverty, war, and racism:

We are here again to protest a growing war. Since it is a very bad war, we acquire the habit of thinking that it must be caused by very bad men. But we only conceal reality. . . . We must simply observe, and quite plainly say, that this coalition, this blitzkrieg, and this demand for acquiescence are creatures, all of them, of a government that since 1932 has considered itself to be fundamentally liberal. . . .

Far from helping Americans to deal with this truth, the anti-communist ideology merely tries to disguise it so that things may stay the way they are. Thus it depicts our presence in other lands not as coercion, but as protection. . . .

This is the action of *corporate liberalism*. It performs for the state a function quite like what the Church once performed for the feudal state. It seeks to justify its burdens and protect it from change.[67]

As a result of this disillusionment, many of the leaders of SDS moved away from the "realignment" strategy toward an emphasis on building a "third party" of radicals, and the analysis of "local insurgency" in *America and the New Era,* and the Hayden strategy of community organizing, provided the theoretical and strategic basis for this effort.[68] Not all of the leadership agreed with the emphasis on neighborhood issues and the nonelectoral focus of the community organizing strategy, however, and there were other SDS projects besides ERAP. Referring to the ERAP approach as "ghetto jumping," Steve Max argued that the solution to poverty could only come through political decisions taken by those in power, and that SDS should concentrate on building *political* organizations in local communities that would participate in electoral activity:

What is entailed here is the building of block-by-block, district-by-district political organizations; not splinter groups or protest movements, but an organization which makes a direct assault in the dominant party, through the primary election.[69]

Those who shared this analysis, as well as those who retained faith in the "realignment" strategy, formed the Political Education Project in 1964 to initiate SDS activity in the elections that year. Although representing a minority of the leadership, they were mandated to function as a project of SDS and given a formal status similar to ERAP. After the sellout at the convention, and with the escalation of the war, support for PEP declined, and it was denied organizational funding the next year.

A third project was the Peace Research and Education Project, which concentrated on preparing and circulating materials on foreign policy issues. Unlike the PEP leaders, the PREP people basically supported the ERAP strategy, but saw a need to continue education on foreign policy even in that context. Headed by Dick Flacks and Paul Booth, the PREP project operated mainly as an internal education vehicle until the formation, in later years, of the Radical Education Project. They did, however, act as the main proponents of activity against the escalating US involvement in Vietnam, and in 1965 became involved in a dispute with ERAP people about whether or not to organize a national antiwar demonstration.

In the years immediately following Port Huron, then, the SDS leaders attempted to develop programs and strategies to operationalize the values that they had defined in the *Port Huron Statement.* The lack of an historical and economic analysis of the origins of those values, of an historical "self-consciousness," led them to base these programs and strategies on their own individual experiences and backgrounds. Without an agreed upon and shared historical analysis, different strategies and programs could make equal claims to validity and to the organization's resources, and the result was a variety of programs whose analytical implications and validity were to be tested in practice. As one leader described it:

If anyone wanted to create an action program, they could call themselves a project, establish some kind of office, and begin to work intensively on that—and whatever budget there was, you'd get it, or a piece of it. . . . It was a way of giving factions . . . a piece of the organization, and letting them try it. The theory being that people should experiment, they shouldn't just argue over their factional positions.[70]

Toward a New Left Paradigm

The attempt of the SDS activists to develop a theory of political activity to guide their efforts was, then, in part a response to other possible alternatives. The initial disenchantment with the Old Left, and the growing disenchantment with liberalism, generated a "theoretical crisis" for the emerging New Left. If the Marxism of the Old Left and the liberalism of the establishment were both discredited by the practice of their proponents, where was the social and political theory embodying the values of the new activists that could provide understanding and direction? The first tentative answer was that no blueprint existed, but that a new theory would emerge out of the practical struggles in which radicals participated. If the intellectuals had no answers, perhaps the "people" did. The Cuban revolution and the civil-rights movement both represented the triumph of *will* over theory, and perhaps if radicals only concentrated on getting the "masses" in motion, the masses would develop their own theory. With this leap of faith, the New Left had come full circle in its quest for collective self-definition.

The individuals who came together in search of collective definitions in the early days of SDS were conscious of themselves only as students whose values differed from those that seemed to characterize existing institutions. To explain this difference, they argued that the structure of university life generated opposition to dominant values. To find hope that their values might be realizable, they distinguished themselves from an Old Left that had failed. In order to find a strategy for change they developed an analysis of power that projected an alliance of the powerless. With the failure of liberalism in power, they developed an explanation of liberalism-as-pure-ideology that led them to an emphasis on practice rather than theory. Without an awareness of the historical process that generated their opposition, however, these ingredients remained unintegrated, personalized, and, ultimately, responsive only to immediate "experience."

Thus, the attempt to develop a theoretical articulation of the self-directed values of the SDS leaders led (as the *Port Huron Statement* illustrates) to a piecemeal "theory" that saw centralized organization as corrupting, individual political action as both an end and a means, and students as a key force in building a New Left. In *America and the New Era,* and with the formation of ERAP in 1963, the notion of "powerlessness" as the common basis for collective political action was added to the theoretical pie. The result was not only an emphasis in practice on eliminating and avoiding formal organizational forms, but also the emergence of anarchism and voluntarism as central features of the ideological development taking place within the organization.

The view of centralized and bureaucratic power as a source of injustice not only meant that organizational forms of the New Left should avoid centralization and bureaucracy, but it also implied that the political objective of a New Left was something *other than* a seizure of state power and the direction of that power on behalf of the "powerless." On the contrary, the objective was the break-up and decentralization of state power to involve more and more people in the decisions affecting their lives. The example of *will* found in the Cuban revolution and the civil-rights movement, and the belief that theory would emerge from action, reinforced a belief in the primacy of the individual as over and against society—a central tenet of anarchism.[71] The implicit priority on "personal experience" as the source of knowledge also fostered voluntarist beliefs that individuals did not have to be presented with "ideology"; common experiences would lead to common theories.

In the ERAP projects, this voluntarism was coupled with populism in the notion that not only would theory emerge from the collective political action of powerless people creating their own organizations, but that whatever theories they developed would be "true." The practical result was that these projects increasingly focused on localized, specific grievances, rather than the structural causes of those grievances. Key ERAP slogans like "Let the people decide" and "A whole lot of people together is strong" were turned against the organizers to justify provincialism and racism, and, in the end, these projects, which had started out as the most radical edge of the New Left, remained ideologically dormant as the whole movement shifted to the left.[72]

Not only did this voluntarism not lead to the generation of a new social and political theory by the "people," but it also operated to maintain a leadership elite rather than produce new leaders. For the fact of the matter was that the initial SDS elite *did* possess theoretical as well as experiential knowledge, and the anti-intellectual and voluntarist strains that appeared in the ERAP projects served only to keep the elite knowledgeable and the newer members in relative ignorance. In ERAP, as in the SDS as a whole, the attempt to develop a theory and a practice that could avoid the "iron law of oligarchy" led toward anarchist theory, and toward manipulative practice. The effort to build a decentralized alliance of "powerless" groups, moreover, led not to a broadening of the institutional framework of the New Left, but to the fragmentation of the existing framework. By the end of 1966, rather than a single "interracial movement of the poor" comprised of poor blacks, poor whites, and a student left, the "movement" was divided into a black movement, a student movement, an antiwar movement, and some local organizations of poor whites—each of which had its own organizational forms, and each of which was sharply split over theory and practice.

This was not, of course, simply a result of the theory developed in the New Left. On the contrary, that theory was a reflection upon the experiences of the individuals involved. Theory developed in response to other paradigms such as the Old Left paradigm and the liberal paradigm, but it was concrete individuals who responded to those other paradigms. And to understand *why* they responded the way they did, it is necessary to examine in more detail both the experiences and the personal background that shaped their actions.

5 On Practice

The SLID leaders of the fifties were often children of immigrants whose sole extracurricular involvements were with the SLID and/or the YPSL.[1] Most of them seem to have gone on to careers in academia or law, and they attended college either in New York, Boston, at Yale, or at the University of Wisconsin.[2] Given the political climate of the time, of course, the absence of other extracurricular involvement may merely reflect the lack of other options once they became involved in left politics.

The SDS leaders of the early sixties exhibited a very different pattern. Of the sixteen leaders elected at Port Huron, three had been student body presidents, three had been editors of their campus newspapers, six had been members of student government, five had been local or national officers of the National Student Association, and almost all had been active in NSA activities.[3] Only three of them had active backgrounds in YPSL, and two or three others had been active in other Old Left organizations.[4] While many of the Port Huron participants were "red diaper babies" (children of old leftists), the most common ties were to SNCC, NSA, or similar groups not connected with the Old Left.

The NSA background of many SDS leaders, like the ties to SNCC, were not accidental. They resulted from the calculated policy followed by Al Haber of lobbying within, and recruiting from, the annual NSA Student Congress. In May of 1961, he had proposed to the LID that SDS should organize a "Liberal Study Group" at the NSA Student Congress scheduled for August at the University of Wisconsin.[5] In his view, the study group would serve as a counter to the organized right, could promote SDS recruitment of new members, and, in general, could make the SDS visible as a center for left-liberal activity. During June and July, he involved other groups in the planning of the study group, such as the Campus Americans for Democratic Action, Student Peace Union, and various campus political parties,[6] and a number of future SDS leaders made contact with the organization during this period. The success of the effort led to a continuation of the LSG at future congresses, and the NSA remained a key source of members and legitimacy for the SDS in the early sixties. One SDS leader stated the relationship bluntly:

We owe NSA our entry to the campus moderate liberals, which they can close off by not inviting us to speak at their regional conferences, to serve on their NEC, or whatever the NSA establishment does . . . they can unilaterally make SDS a sectarian Left organization by so classifying it with YPSL and YSA, et. al. The legitimate organizations are NSM, SNCC, ADA, and us, and we must remain one of them.[7]

The close relationship with SNCC was also not accidental. As early as the Human Rights in the North Conference, in the Spring of 1960, Haber had begun cultivating relationships with SNCC leaders. Tim Jenkins was elected to the SDS-NEC in 1961, and he was both an NSA national affairs vice-president, and a founder of SNCC. Sandra Cason Hayden, another NEC member, worked with SNCC, while Bob Zellner was active with CORE. Both Tom Hayden and Paul Potter (the latter on behalf of NSA) traveled with SNCC workers in late 1961 and early 1962, and in May 1962, Hayden organized a conference on "Race and Politics" at the University of North Carolina.[8] At the Port Huron convention, at least five persons with close ties to SNCC were seated as delegates.

In a larger sense, however, these formal ties to the NSA and SNCC do not explain the composition of the SDS in the early sixties. The conscious recruitment policy Haber followed from 1960 on was responsible for making the SDS visible as a *possible* center for student activity on the left, but it was not responsible for generating the interest in such activity. Indeed, one of the central characteristics of the Port Huron generation of SDS leaders was that they came to the organization already involved in local political organizing. Tom Hayden not only had been editor of the *Michigan Daily,* but he also helped create the VOICE political party. At Oberlin, Paul Potter and Rennie Davis had formed the Progressive Student League in 1960-61; Paul Booth and Rebecca Adams were active in the Swarthmore Political Action Club; Todd Gitlin was a leader of Tocsin at Harvard; and at the University of Chicago, Clark Kissinger was chairman of POLIT.[9]

For these students, the raw "experiences" so essential to their attempt to understand the source of their discontent were provided by participation in these local activities. What SDS offered was an opportunity for them to get together with others similarly involved in order to seek an intellectual foundation for defining the meaning and significance of common experiences. In this early period SDS was not the source of political programs and activities for students to join, but rather a kind of "think-tank" where activists could seek a larger analysis of their personal involvement. Unlike the Student Peace Union, the SDS was not created in order to implement a political strategy, but began as an attempt to develop a political strategy, and because of this SDS as an organization developed as a kind of extension of the particular individuals involved. As one of the early leaders recalled the nature of this process in 1962-63:

The way SDS presented itself in Cambridge that year . . . was as the place that activists from other movements went to talk. . . . And the password that year . . .

was that the issues were interrelated. So . . . the Cambridge organizer saw it as his job to bring civil rights and other activists together and sit them down at a table, and have them recognize themselves as belonging to a common movement. But SDS itself was not to be for action.[10]

The Formation of an "Elite"

Earlier, I referred to the group of SDS leaders who became active in the organization around the time of the Port Huron convention as an "elite." In using that term, I seek to convey not only the fact that, collectively, they controlled the decision-making machinery of SDS, but also that they tended to act as a cohesive group toward other members of the organization. The period that culminated, roughly, with the Port Huron convention was when the bonds that united them were forged, and the *Port Huron Statement* was an attempt to articulate the shared definitions that emerged from their interaction. This process of group formation was, however, only in a very limited sense related to the *formal* organizational structure of SDS.

Instead, the formation of this "elite" was mainly an informal process that began at the University of Michigan around 1960. Al Haber had already been active in the Political Issues Club and in the "beat" culture on the fringes of the campus. Dick Flacks became a graduate student in social psychology at Michigan in 1958, having already "dropped out" of the Labor Youth League, and Tom Hayden was an undergraduate from 1957 to 1961. Hayden joined the staff of the *Michigan Daily* in his first year on campus and became editor of the paper in 1960. During the summer of 1960 he traveled to Berkeley, where he spent considerable time with SLATE leaders, after which he covered the Democratic convention for the paper, and finally attended the NSA Student Congress in Minnesota.[11] In the fall, he wrote a series of long articles on "student social action" in which he called for a new student movement. At the NSA Congress, Hayden met some of the southern students working with SNCC (including his first wife) and later met Haber during picket demonstrations in Ann Arbor supporting the sit-in campaign.[12]

Shortly thereafter, Haber and Hayden began a kind of ongoing debate, mostly through correspondence, on the best way to build the new student movement both of them desired. Haber argued that SDS could be the vehicle for developing such a movement, while Hayden favored creating a new organization, and at issue was the relationship such a movement should have with the Old Left. Hayden was skeptical of any such relationship:

We had a kind of running debate, because my inclination was that a new organization should be formed, partly because . . . I really didn't believe there should be any continuity with the Old Left whatsoever, and I really believed that we were born fresh out of our own experience and that it would be a burden to become involved at all with the history of the left.[13]

By the fall of 1961, Hayden agreed to give SDS a chance, and was hired as a field staff working out of Atlanta. Through carbon copies of their letters, the two began to extend their network to others with similar sentiments, and for several years after Port Huron this method of communication set the pattern for the exchange of ideas among the elite. From contacts made at the NSA Student Congress the network was extended to include Paul Booth and Rebecca Adams at Swarthmore, Robb Burlage at Texas (soon to go to Harvard), and Paul Potter and Rennie Davis at Oberlin. Each of these was involved in political activity at his or her own school, primarily around civil-rights issues, but all shared the desire for a broader student movement that could provide a framework for their own work. What brought them together initially was not a specific program for building such a movement, but rather a structure of sentiments that was better expressed in "values" or "feelings" than in traditional political language. Hayden described his own feelings as moving from a kind of "beatnik" alienation toward a sense that structural change was possible:

Being "beat" is kind of having an alienation from the world to begin with . . . and that came in the fifties. It was not a period when there were eye-opening events that outraged you. No, these values were pretty shattered, and it was more a matter of coming to believe in action. For me, that was the main struggle—not overcoming belief in America and belief in conventional action. It was a matter of coming out of feeling isolated and beginning to believe that something was possible.[14]

In terms of family background, the members of the SDS elite were a diverse group. Hayden's father was an accountant in Michigan, and he was raised as a Catholic; Paul Potter's father was a farmer; Bob Ross's a garment worker; Lee Webb's a laborer. Paul Booth, Rennie Davis, and Richard Rothstein all had fathers who had been federal civil servants, while Todd Gitlin's parents were high-school teachers. The fathers of Robb Burlage and Al Haber were university professors, while Betty Garman's was a corporation executive. Sharon Jeffrey's mother was a political and labor leader in Michigan, while Steve Max's father was an ex-editor of the *Worker*.[15] Politically, too, the members of the elite were a mixed group. Several (e.g., Max, Flacks, and Ross) were already radicals when they met the others and had been exposed to the Old Left; others (e.g., Hayden, Haber, and Gitlin) were first "beatniks" before turning seriously to political activity; while still others (e.g., Davis and Potter) were more typical "liberals" who became gradually radicalized as a result of their experiences.

Despite this variety in background, all of them felt the isolation that Hayden described, and political activity became a vehicle for developing a shared "identity" that overshadowed the differences. The *PHS* definition of politics as having the function "of bringing men out of isolation and into community" was an apt statement of their own experience. What they shared, at first, was not an analysis or program, but an *experience* of personal liberation through political activity. The intensity of the Port Huron Convention and the traumatic fight with the LID that followed deepened the personal bonds by providing, in addition to *similar* experiences of a *similar* process, *common* experiences of a *shared* process.

The *Port Huron Statement* was an attempt to articulate a common set of definitions of these experiences, but that attempt has sometimes been misinterpreted. The values spelled out in the PHS were not merely negative ones—antiauthoritarianism, antielitism, nonexclusion, antibureaucratic. On the contrary, they also stressed a positive desire for self-direction, community, creativity, and participation. In trying to articulate these values, and to embody them in practice, however, the members of the elite were constrained by the particular circumstances that brought them together.

More specifically, the crystallization of these values into consciously articulated form was precipitated by the civil-rights movement. Most of the early SDS leaders met one another in the context of developing support for the southern students, and their early efforts were directed toward identifying and articulating what it was about the civil-rights movement they found appealing. Their conclusion seemed to be that it was the kind of personal relationships fostered within the movement that were so appealing, rather than the specific practical objectives put forth as demands. The *Port Huron Statement* saw the civil-rights movement as heartening because it indicated "that there can be a passage out of apathy," and in describing their contacts with the movement, the SDS activists emphasized the sense of community and self-determination that characterized relationships within the southern movement.[16] What they found appealing was that people whose lives had been controlled by others, and who had for so long conformed to the expectations of white Americans, were taking the direction of their lives into their own hands—and the result seemed to be "better" human relationships among those involved.

Out of this initial emotional identification with the civil-rights movement came two errors that were crucial in the failure of the New Left to develop an historical self-consciousness. The first error was that the students projected the values that lay behind *their* discontent onto the civil-rights movement, and in the process confused the historically specific configuration of values that moved them with universal values of Reason and Humanism.[17] If these same universal values were at the root of both their own dis-content and the civil-rights movement, then the explanation for these values must lie in the similarities of the two movements, rather than in any differences. The immediate consequence of this kind of reasoning was that when the SDS activists sought to develop a strategy for social change distinct from the strategies of the Old Left and of liberals, they rooted their strategy not in an analysis of their own class origins, but in an analysis of their shared "powerlessness" with blacks and the poor.

The second error was related to the first, and consisted of the mistaken equation of the *objectives* of the civil-rights movement with their own objectives. Since these universal values were at the root of both movements, then the objective of both must be the restructuring of social institutions to embody those values. What the students did not see was that the nonviolent philosophy and the styles of personal interaction in the civil-rights movement were *means* to an end—but the end, itself, was a redistribution of power and wealth in American society. This confusion of means and ends had the short-term effect of sharpening the radical *political* thrust of the New Left, because they equated the realization of their objectives with the success of the civil-rights movement. In later years, however, when the development of the black movement led to the abandonment of nonviolence and the adoption of disciplined organizational forms in order to achieve its objective, many New Left activists were unwilling to go along. Indeed, these same issues occupied a central place in the factional struggles that fragmented the New Left.

Nevertheless, in 1961 and 1962, the SDS elite did equate the aims and objectives of the civil-rights movement with their own aims and objectives, and this identification was a crucial factor both to the kind of analysis the New Left developed and to the style of organizing they engaged in. The activities of the young SNCC workers, in particular, came to serve as a model of the kind of organizing and the form of organization the SDS leaders sought to emulate. The SDS elite brought to that task, however, their own very special characteristics, and the results were very different from what they envisioned.

Decision Making and Organizational Structure

The process by which the SDS elite came to articulate a set of shared values, and the forms of their political activity, were informal and deeply personalized, combining direct participation with intellectual reflection and debate until consensus was achieved. Their backgrounds as "student leaders" also meant, however, that these students had mastered the parliamentary forms of their high schools and colleges, and when it came to creating a formal structure for the SDS, they did not attempt to develop an organizational form that reflected their own style of political activity, but instead (and seemingly without question) adopted a typical hierarchical form with levels of committees, staff, and officers each with designated authority and responsibility.

The point is not that a parliamentary form was a "bad" form (an argument that gained popularity in later years), but that it did not coincide with their own pattern of decision making and activity. The result, rather quickly, was that the formal structure of SDS had little to do with how decisions were actually made. In formal terms, the Port Huron convention elected a president (Tom Hayden), a vice-president (Paul Booth), a national secretary, a field secretary, and a National Executive Committee —all with designated responsibilities and authority. Informally, those members of the NEC who were part of the "elite"—with Hayden as first among equals-carried on intense discussions and debates among themselves, and when they reached consensus decisions followed. The members of the SDS elite were highly sensitive to the tendency of organizations to follow an "iron law of oligarchy," and it was assumed from the outset that officers would not run for reelection.[18] The members of the elite were also leaders, however, and their qualities of leadership did not disappear when they no longer held formal office.

Although Tom Hayden stepped down as president at the 1963 convention (to be replaced by Todd Gitlin), he remained the dominant figure in the elite that ran the organization.[19] Similarly, although new faces appeared among the staff and National Council in 1963 and 1964, the old elite continued to control the organization from its roots in strong local chapters,[20] and through its identification with the *PHS* (whose sentiments had attracted many of the newer members). The real effect of the emphasis on rotation of leaders was to make the actual leaders of the organization unaccountable to the members in terms of the formal structure.

The attitude of the elite toward the formal structure was, at best, ambivalent. For the most part, they did not wish to formally hold office as staff members—and thus be accountable for the routine tasks such work required—but they continued to direct the organization through their local activity and through the informal network among themselves. As early as the end of 1963, this impotence of the formal structure began the dissolution of representative structures in the organization. When a National Council was formed, the members of the NEC decided that they should only function as "at-large" members of the NC, and the elected NEC ceased to function as a decision-making body.[21] The rationale for this was, of course, that the National Council was a larger body, and thus more members would be involved in directing the organization. As time went on, the notion of "elected, voting" members was deemed "elitist," and all who attended meetings of the National Council were assumed to have a right to vote.[22]

The impact of this trend was twofold. First, as decision-making bodies became larger and larger, it meant that small, organized groups within them could have influence out of proportion to their numbers because the others were unorganized; this encouraged both "packing" meetings and factionalism. Second, since such bodies could only meet infrequently, it meant that day-to-day control of the *policies* (as well as the administration) of the organization increasingly was concentrated in the national staff. In the late sixties, the offices of president and vice-president were abolished, and the de facto control by the national staff was formally recognized in a revised constitution. [23]

The full impact of this gap between form and practice began to be felt with the creation of the ERAP project. During the first year and a half following its inception, the organizational structure of the project was steadily separated from accountability to the rest of the organization. While the SDS national office remained in New York, a national ERAP office was established in Ann Arbor, and Rennie Davis was appointed national director of ERAP with the authority to appoint project directors of local ERAP projects and raise funds independent of SDS. [24] Although the SDS National Council elected a committee to supervise ERAP, the national ERAP staff and local project directors constituted a majority of that committee. In September of 1964, the ERAP project was granted authority to initiate new local projects without prior authorization of the NC, and in 1965 the ERAP project abolished its own national office in favor of total local autonomy. [25]

This separation between SDS structures and the ERAP project reflected the view of the ERAP organizers that SDS (as a student organization) and ERAP (as an organization of the poor) were two distinct components of the New Left they hoped to build. One of the guiding documents of ERAP, written in the winter of 1963, makes this view clear:

The SDS national staff, working closely with the ERAP and PREP staffs, would need to continue campus education and action programming. . . . Structurally, this means SDS would become the student movement tied to ERAP and PREP but also a movement within the student community itself. . . . If from this there eventually flows a more integrated organization, a Movement for a Democratic Society . . . that will be determined by social and psychological developments that are difficult to predict. [26]

Thus, ERAP was viewed as an attempt to broaden the base of a New Left beyond its initial student composition. Most of the SDS elite not only supported the ERAP development, but actually participated in local projects—and this is what made the separation so important. At first, many of them continued to play active roles in the SDS—attending National

Council meetings, serving on committees, writing articles, etc.—while at the same time becoming peripherally involved in local projects. As time passed, however, they began to withdraw from the SDS structures and, indeed, the meetings of the ERAP National Committee (in terms of the individuals attending and the issues discussed) looked like the early meetings of the SDS National Executive Committee at the time of the Port Huron convention. [27] In withdrawing from the SDS structures, they made no effort to "train" a new group of leaders to replace them, and with the dissolution of the national ERAP office, even the contact and exchange that marked their own interactions broke down. By 1965, it is probably fair to say that the "elite" that had guided the organization since before Port Huron no longer constituted a cohesive group.

Because the SDS elite never developed an historical analysis to ground its vision of a New Left, the strategic and structural implications of the elite's practice were never debated in the context of a theory of social change. Instead, the strategy issues were, themselves, raised to the level of fundamental issues. Implicit differences in theory became embodied in different strategies, which in turn became embodied in separate organizational structures (ERAP, PEP, PREP), and these different projects then contested for support from the national convention and National Council by proposing different "strategies" and "priorities." The dispute between ERAP and PEP was not discussed in terms of an analysis of the "agency" of change in American society that flowed from an analysis of the sources and dynamics of change, but rather as a debate between "ghetto jumping" and "liberalism." [28] The relationship between ERAP and SDS, similarly, was not considered in terms of the social forces generating a New Left, but as a choice between "campus" organizing and "community" organizing.

In the summer of 1964, several hundred students from the North went to Mississippi to participate in the SNCC-initiated Mississippi Summer Project, and the experiences of those students made history. Although considerably less publicized, that same summer the SDS-ERAP project placed 125 student organizers in the nine urban areas of the North. [29] By the end of the summer, most of the members of the SDS elite were either involved in the ERAP projects or in PEP efforts to organize support for the MFDP at the Democratic convention, and by early fall the main center of SDS activity seemed to have decidedly moved off campus. These involvements not only shaped the attitudes of the elite toward the SDS as a whole, but increased internal divisions within the elite by exposing them to different kinds of "experiences." With the sudden and rapid growth in membership of SDS during 1965, and the shift in issues that fostered that growth, the cohesiveness and the power of the original elite was shattered, and the character and direction of the organization was fundamentally altered.

A Changing of the Guard

At the time of the 1963 SDS convention, the organization had about fourteen functioning chapters and under 1000 members.[30] By the 1964 convention, membership had only grown to about 1200 members in some twenty-seven chapters.[31] By June of 1965, the organization had mushroomed to more than 4000 members in over 125 chapters.[32] In the span of that one school year the SDS had more than tripled in size, yet, this rapid growth was not an outgrowth of activities by the key "projects" the elite had created.

Instead, the dramatic growth came as a response to two "new" issues. The first of these concerned the oppressive character of university life, which became the central focus of the Free Speech Movement at Berkeley in the fall of 1964. Led by students who had gone to Mississippi during the summer, the FSM demonstrated the potential appeal of student syndicalism as an issue to mobilize and "radicalize" college students. What began as an attempt to exercise the same rights of free speech and political activity that they had demanded for southern blacks soon mushroomed into a broad attack on the "bureaucratic" and "factory-like" character of large universities. Here, too, the opposition to change was led by liberals, this time in the person of Clark Kerr.

In 1963 the chancellor of Berkeley gave a series of lectures on *The Uses of the University,* in which he argued that the university existed to meet the changing needs of society, and that the increasingly central role of knowledge in the growth and development of business and government required that the university adapt itself to the needs of these institutions.[33] The emergence of the "multiversity," he argued, required that principles of rational administration be applied to all sectors of university life, and he saw the university president as the central figure in this reorganization. "Persuasion" was the key weapon of this new type of administrator, whose task was to make the university run smoothly.

And yet, when the FSM protests began, persuasion was quickly abandoned in favor of threats and the use of police. The contradiction between liberal rhetoric and practice were not lost on the Berkeley students, and the lesson they learned was succintly stated by Mario Savio during the Sproul Hall sit-in:

One conception of the university, suggested by a classical Christian formulation, is that it be in the world but not of the world. The conception of Clark Kerr by contrast is that the university is part and parcel of this particular stage in the history of American society; it stands to serve the needs of American industry; it is a factory that turns out a product needed by industry or government. . . . It can permit two kinds of speech: speech which encourages continuation of the status quo, and speech which advocates changes in it so radical as to be irrelevant in the foreseeable future. . . . Speech with consequences, speech in the area of civil rights, speech which some might regard as illegal, must stop.[34]

During the FSM protests,[35] more than eight hundred students were arrested, more than five thousand students regularly attended mass meetings, and the students were able to effectively close down the university until most of their original demands were met. More important, the FSM protests aroused sympathy and support on campuses across the country, and within two years, "student power" became a central focus of student activity everywhere.

The SDS national office spread the message of the Berkeley students to other campuses and organized support demonstrations during the fall. Moreover, the SDS began to organize similar protests at other "multiversities," sending FSM documents and speakers to help local chapters organize demonstrations. The national office also initiated a "university reform" project to coordinate the new SDS thrust on campus.

The second major issue that spurred the growth in membership was the escalation of the war in Vietnam. As early as February of 1964 the PREP project had sent out a special mailing on the "New Crisis in Vietnam," forecasting a major escalation of US involvement,[36] and during that year PREP attempted to disseminate information on the war to the SDS mailing list. At a meeting of the National Council in December of 1964, the PREP people proposed a spring March on Washington to call for an end to the war, but a fierce debate ensued, with many of the ERAP leaders opposing the idea as both a waste of organizational resources and a bad strategy for building a movement.[37] Although the proposal was first voted down, the meeting later reconsidered and approved the proposal.

The march was called for April 17, 1965, and the SDS analysis of the war was summarized in six points: the war was fundamentally a civil war; it was a losing war because of popular support for the NLF; it was a self-defeating war because US involvement would lead to even greater instability in Southeast Asia; it was a dangerous war because it risked intervention by the Soviet Union and China; it was an undeclared war that wasted resources that should be spent on abolishing poverty in America; and it was an immoral war in which the US engaged in murder.[38] In their preparations for the march, the organizers came to grips with the criticism that marches were a futile gesture. They identified three kinds of past marches: those that attempted to accomplish definite legislative or policy objectives (like the 1963 March on Washington for Jobs and Freedom); those that intended to focus public attention on specific situations with less defined goals (like the Selma march); and those that were designed to demonstrate the commitment and concern of the marchers (like the traditional Easter peace walks).[39]

The SDS organizers noted that the first of these strategies assumed the responsiveness of government to protest, an assumption they were not prepared to make. The second type of march, they argued, was subject to manipulation and deals because it lacked any long-term objectives. They criticized the third type because it was not directed to activities after the march was over. The April march, in contrast to these earlier types, had a different purpose: first, it was designed to break the "manipulated consensus" behind the war policy; second, it was designed to initiate a debate on the *issues* of the war and thus bring into the public domain political issues that had been handled by private manipulation; and finally, the march was aimed at uniting the "insurgent" groups who were the domestic victims of the war because of wasted resources and similar manipulation here at home.[40]

The April march also had one other feature that distinguished it from earlier protests, and that was the determination of the SDS organizers that no political tendency would be excluded from participation. For the first time in the postwar period, Communists were accorded the same status and rights as anti-Communist and non-Communist political groups, and this policy led the LID to protest the march and SANE to refuse participation. The spectacular success of the march, however, (some 25,000 persons participated) provided strong justification for the SDS position that anticommunism on the left was no longer a condition for political relevance. Indeed, when SANE called for another march in November around the slogan "Negotiate Now," SDS president Carl Oglesby brought the long-simmering disenchantment with anti-Communist liberals into the open with a speech that named "corporate liberalism" as the "system" responsible for war abroad and poverty at home.

The success of the April march made SDS *the* visible center for national antiwar activity and, together with the visibility gained during its support of the FSM, led to the sharp growth in membership during 1965. Ironically, at precisely the moment when the organization was fulfilling Haber's vision of the SDS as the "national center" for a new student left, the contradictions that had been building in the theory and practice of the elite culminated in its disintegration as a cohesive force and led to a paralysis of the organization. Most of the elite remained aloof from the antiwar activities, both because they saw it drawing attention and energy away from the plight of the domestic poor, and because their deep involvement in ERAP work left them little time for other activities. This attitude was reflected in the decision of the 1965 convention to reaffirm the organization's commitment to community organizing and multi-issue politics, and to consciously reject taking the leadership of the antiwar movement.[41]

Despite this reaffirmation by the convention, the same considerations that led the elite to oppose antiwar activities also led those in ERAP projects to refuse election as officers or even (with few exceptions) membership on the National Council. The result was that those persons in the best position to lead the SDS in its chosen course of action were unavailable. And if this were not enough, the four hundred convention delegates also voted to weaken the powers of the president and abolish (temporarily) the office of national secretary, so that no program could be effectively carried out even by the new leaders.

In certain respects the SDS had come full circle by 1966 and resembled the organization of 1962; new leaders assumed power and were critical of those who had guided the organization in previous years, while the latter seemed to have failed in the goals they set for themselves. The organization that began as an attempt to build a student left but later moved off campus to organize an interracial movement of the poor, by 1966 had returned to its campus roots. Unlike the experience of the early sixties, however, the disintegration of the SDS elite—and of the theory and practice they represented—did not lead to a broadening and unifying of the New Left, but instead was followed by a fragmenting process of single-issue organizing in which the gap between theory and practice grew even greater.

In the latter half of the sixties, the Students for a Democratic Society grew in numbers and influence, while at the same time it changed in composition and direction. By the end of the decade, literally tens of thousands of students had been exposed to radical political ideas through the SDS, and the organization had played a major role in shattering the political stagnation of the fifties. In spite of this later growth, however, the ultimate decline of the SDS was already foreshadowed in the failure of the SDS elite to develop, in addition to political beliefs, an historical understanding of their own discontent.

In Search of Historical Self-Consciousness

During its formative years, the theory and practice of the SDS developed as a response to the theory and practice of competing paradigms of social change, in particular, to an Old Left paradigm and a liberal paradigm. What this process represented was the formation of a *political* "identity" by the young activists. This development was part of a larger process, however; the quest for an *historical* identity. The articulation of shared values, and the development of strategies and programs based on those values, provided an analysis of *how* this New Left was different from an earlier left and from liberals, but there remained the nagging question of *why* they were different. Just as the formation of a political identity was affected by their immediate contact with alternative political identities, the quest for an historical identity was shaped by the immediate social institutions with which they had contact.

More specifically, their primary social identity was rooted in their role as *students*. As political activists, however, they represented a small minority of the college students of their time, and in attempting to understand why it was that most students remained ''apathetic'' toward political activity, they turned their attention, first, to an examination of university life:

But apathy is not simply an attitude; it is a product of social institutions, and of the structure and organization of higher education itself. The extracurricular life is ordered according to *in loco parentis* theory, which ratifies the Administration as the moral guardian of the young. . . . The university ''prepares'' the student for ''citizenship'' through perpetual rehearsals and, usually, through emasculation of what creative spirit there is in the individual. . . .

Further, academia includes a radical separation of students from the material of study . . . The specialization of function and knowledge . . . has produced an exaggerated compartmentalization of study and understanding. . . .

There is, finally, the cumbersome academic bureaucracy. . . . The size and financing systems of the university enhance the permanent trusteeship of the administrative bureaucracy, their power leading to a shift of the value standards of business and administrative mentality within the university. . . .

The real function of the educational system—as opposed to its more rhetorical function of ''searching for truth''—is to impart the key information and styles that will help the student get by, modestly but comfortably, in the big society beyond.[42]

Despite all this, it seemed to them that the university might also be the place to begin a struggle for change. They argued that the university was located in a permanent position of social influence; that it was the central institution for organizing and transmitting knowledge; that it was closely tied by defense contracts and social science consulting to government and business, and because of this any change in the university would have effects elsewhere in society; and finally, that the university was the only institution open to participation by individuals of widely divergent viewpoints.

What this reflected was a view of themselves not only as students in a general sense, but as ''intellectuals'' in particular, and their choice of the university as the place to begin a radical movement was greatly influenced by C. Wright Mills's suggestion that, in modern society, intellectuals were a key agency of social change:

It is with this problem of agency in mind that I have been studying . . . the intellectuals, as a possible, immediate, radical agency of change. . . .

In the first place, is it not clear that if we try to be realistic in our utopianism . . . a writer in our countries on the left today *must* begin with the intellectuals? For that is what we are, that is where we stand.[43]

This dual identity as both students and intellectuals was difficult to maintain, since it was precisely as intellectuals that they found student life in the modern university most stultifying. Their own creative instincts and desire for self-direction found an outlet in the civil-rights movement and in political activity, and these channels were far more tempting than concentrating their efforts within the confines of the mass university. By the time of *America and the New Era,* their thinking had shifted toward a rejection of their student identity, and they sought an analysis of how "intellectuals" might link up with other social groups in a movement for change:

It has been clear that *independent, political* participation by intellectuals in the political process has been officially resisted and successfully undermined. . . . It is the grim irony of the Fifties that the supposed centers of innovation in the social system provided the manpower and organizational facilities which lubricated the efficient operation of the military industrial complex.

This structure of quiescence is beginning to break down. The development of the civil rights movement and other centers of independent insurgency has for the first time since the war created centers of power outside the university, to which intellectuals could turn for creative as well as political involvement. . . . The bureaucratic and ideological structures of . . . liberal education have been penetrated; and with this breakout of significant numbers of students and intellectuals has come . . . an independence, a sense of power and mobility which promise to have deep and long-ranging effects on the university system as well as on the emergent centers of power in the social order.[44]

The implication of this analysis was clear; the role for concerned intellectuals was active participation in the struggles of "insurgent" groups. Although *ANE* allowed a role for students, as students, by suggesting that they provide the information and research needed by insurgent groups, the SDS leaders chose to abandon the student identity and participate directly as intellectuals. This identity as intellectuals also proved difficult to maintain, however, when the regular contacts in the ERAP projects were with people with little education who could not afford the luxury of dealing with ideas in the abstract. Just as the dual identity as both students and intellectuals had been uncomfortable in the university setting, the dual identity as intellectuals and "just plain folk" proved uncomfortable in the community organization. Once again, the response of the SDS activists was to reject their earlier identity (as intellectuals), and to seek a new one by submerging themselves in the life of the people they sought to organize. In the ERAP projects, this led to systematic attempts to discourage "intellectualizing" and instead to become "one with the people."[45] With the gradual dissolution of the ERAP projects and the failure of the strategy of building an interracial movement of the poor, no readily available social identity remained, and the members of the initial elite were forced to return to a view of themselves as some kind of "intelligentsia," though with no real analysis to guide their actions.

This convoluted quest was pursued by a relatively small number of New Left activists, however. Most students remained in school and pursued political activity as an adjunct to their studies, and for them the tension between their student identity and political activity remained a problem. The issues raised in the struggles of the FSM offered a possible resolution of this tension, by demonstrating that the same opportunities for creativity and self-direction found in civil rights and community organizing activity also might be found in a campaign to restructure the university. The argument, put simply, was that just as black people were oppressed in the South, students were oppressed in the university, that the *character* of the oppression of university life was not qualitatively different from the oppression of blacks. After reciting, once again, their grievances at the rationalization, bureaucratization, and specialization of university life, the students summed up their attitude toward the modern university:

By identifying the parts of the machinery in our factory, the way in which we have described them, and their blending into our society of institutionalized greed, might lead people to assume that we have a fundamental bias against institutions as such. . . . When we assert that Free Speech and the factory, or politics and education, are bound up together, we are pointing to the obvious. In a twentieth century industrial state, ignorance will be the definition of slavery. If centers of education fail, they will be the producers of the twentieth century slave. To put it in more traditional American terms, popular government cannot survive without education for the people. . . . We must now begin the demand of the right to know. . . . It is ours to demand meaning; we must insist upon meaning.[46]

To those members of the SDS elite who had retained a belief in campus organizing (e.g., Booth, Kissinger, and Flacks), as well as to the new members entering the organization in 1965, the "success" of the FSM and the response it received nationally indicated a way out of the dilemma that was paralyzing the organization. By identifying the university as part and parcel of a system that fostered militarism, racism, and poverty, the students could focus their efforts on the one institution most accessible to their direct actions. By emphasizing the increasing interrelation between knowledge and power in modern society, they could argue that the university was a crucial institution and that change in the university could lead to broader social change. In this return to the university as a locus of political activity, however, they also returned to an analysis that viewed the "distorted" values found in the university as a product of the changing role of the university in society. What they failed to examine was whether or not their own values and their own discontent were generated by those same large-scale changes, rather than by the conditions of student life in the university. Because of this failure, the quest for an historical identity once again stopped with their identity as "students," and the possibility that their discontent (and the values underlying it) reflected the discontent of a broad strata of the population remained hidden from their view.

Part III
Radical Consciousness and
Social Process

The notion of class entails the notion of historical relationship. Like any other relationship, it is a fluency which evades analysis if we attempt to stop it dead at any given moment and anatomise its structure. The finest-meshed sociological net cannot give us a pure specimen of class, any more than it can give us of deference or of love. The relationship must always be embodied in real people and in a real context. . . . And class happens when some men, as a result of common experiences (inherited or shared), feel and articulate the identity of their interests as between themselves, and as against other men whose interests are different from (and usually opposed to) theirs. The class experience is largely determined by the productive relations into which men are born—or enter involuntarily. Class-consciousness is the way in which these experiences are handled in cultural terms: embodied in traditions, value-systems, ideas, and institutional forms. If the experience appears as determined, class consciousness does not.

(E.P. Thompson, *The Making of the English Working Class*)

6

The New Left and American Society

In their critique of the multiversity, the Berkeley students quoted with approval Paul Goodman's assertion that students were not merely marginally alienated as "intellectuals," but that they were, in fact, an exploited *class:*

At present, in the United States, students—middle-class youth—are the major exploited class (Negroes, small farmers, the aged are rather outcast groups—their labor is not needed and they are not wanted). The labor of intelligent youth *is* needed and they are accordingly subjected to tight scheduling, speed up and other factory exploitative methods.[1]

With this assertion, the quest of the New Left for a historical self-consciousness and a social identity moved to a new level of analysis, moved beyond a subjective identification as students and intellectuals toward an attempt to explain the emergence of the New Left as a consequence of objective, material changes in the structure of American society.

As described in previous chapters, the gradual development of a New Left theory and practice in the early years of the sixties involved two related processes: the first was their attempt to define and articulate the features of social and political reality they felt crucial; the second was their attempt to develop meaningful categories for interpreting that reality, and to initiate action based on that interpretation. They saw a world characterized by poverty, racism, and militarism, in which even the most stable and affluent society embodied and perpetuated social inequalities. It was a reality, moreover, in which the price of stability and affluence, even for those it materially benefited, was a steady decrease in the areas of life over which individual actions had influence. Indeed, the very stability of American political life in the fifties made all the more visible problems of poverty, racism, and militarism. The struggles of the Vietnamese, the Hungarians, the Cubans, and (particularly) black Americans, not only dramatized these features of social life; they also suggested that through collective social action individuals could reassert control over their own lives.

As they attempted to understand the forces that shaped this reality and to develop strategies for changing it, they were forced to confront other interpretations of reality and other strategies for change. The Old Left paradigm confronted them as a theory and practice that had failed. The Communist's uncritical support of the Soviet Union supported one side in the continued expansion of the arms race, while the anticommunism of the remainder of the Old Left supported the cold war from the other side. The class analysis of capitalism employed by both, moreover, seemed absurd in the face of the integration of the American labor movement into American capitalism, while it provided no framework for understanding the only visible effort at social change—the southern civil-rights movement.

The liberal paradigm also seemed a theory and practice that had failed, since the New Frontier liberals in power continued the cold war, failed to aid civil-rights movements, and did not attack the problems of poverty.

The theoretical lessons the new activists drew from their contacts with these alternative paradigms were that a class analysis provided no strategy for change, and that power corrupts good intentions. As an alternative paradigm, the New Left developed a theory of centralized power as the source of racism, poverty, and militarism, and projected a strategy of organizing the powerless in an attempt to democratize and decentralize power. After they had *defined* a social reality, and *interpreted* that reality, the New Left activists tried to develop an *understanding* of the sources of their definitions and interpretations. In trying to understand *why* that reality they had defined and interpreted bothered them, they turned to an analysis of values about human nature. In this analysis, they argued that the basis for evaluating social organization and social relationships was the extent to which these relationships allowed and fostered creativity, independence, flexibility, and a desire for community on the part of individuals. In trying to understand why that reality bothered *them*, they turned to an analysis of the character and role of intellectuals as a social group. With the FSM analysis of intellectuals as an exploited class, this effort was transformed from a view of "intellectuals" as an ahistorical and universal category, to a concrete analysis of the dynamic impact of social structure on political thought and behavior.

In locating and interpreting the sources and character of the New Left within changing social structures of American society, previous studies of the New Left paint widely divergent portraits. To evaluate these interpretations, one must move carefully through a forest of subtle distinctions of emphasis and interpretation.

Two quite different emphases seem to differentiate analyses of the New Left. The majority of earlier accounts focus on the notion of "generational conflict" as a central characteristic of New Left opposition. Beginning with the fact that the New Left was comprised of *young* people, these accounts have sought to explain the New Left in terms either of psychological or of social-structural characteristics of modern youth. Thus, while Feuer explains New Left opposition as a process in which universal and deep-rooted psychological traits always characteristic of youth are combined with a special set of historical circumstances that leads to the "deauthoritization" of elders, Keniston and Flacks explain New Left opposition in terms of the emergence of "youth" as a distinct social and social-psychological category in modern society. While there are important differences between the psychological and the structural accounts of New Left opposition, this common focus on generational conflict reflects a belief that membership in the social category of "youth" is a primary variable that accounts for the growth and nature of the New Left.

While notions of generational conflict have been the major focus of academic explanations of the New Left, efforts by activists (both of the Old and New Left) to explain the rise of New Left opposition have emphasized a somewhat different set of categories.

Writers of all political persuasions have discussed the significance of the New Left in relation to classical Marxist notions of "social class," and the conclusions have been as varied as the politics of the authors. Some have assumed that students and intellectuals remain a constituent part of the "bourgeoisie"; thus, the rebellion of the New Left, while (perhaps) progressive, was ultimately bourgeois or petit-bourgeois in its aims. Others have argued that students exist *outside* the political economy of the American system and are therefore capable of becoming a primary revolutionary force in advanced industrial society precisely because they are not subject to the temptations and corruptions of affluence that afflict the white working class.

Still another argument has maintained that students are a primary revolutionary force, because, for the first time, the technological revolution has placed them *inside* the political economy. More recently, Bettina Aptheker has argued that a revolution in the mode of production has altered the structure of the working class in such a way that, for the first time, intellectuals have become a constituent part of the working class.[2]

While these explanations also begin from age-related characteristics of the New Left (its *student* character), they differ from generational conflict explanations in that their focus is on the changing role and function of students and intellectuals *within* the broader social structure, rather than on the more amorphous category of "youth." While generational conflict explanations tend to focus on the common situation and experiences of youth and/or students regardless of their class backgrounds, Marxist and neo-Marxist explanations tend to focus on the characteristics of student life as a manifestation of the class structure.

Two main types of neo-Marxist theories have been advanced to explain the New Left: "new working class" theories and "post-scarcity" theories. The essence of new working class theories is the assertion that the growth of "mass" universities has resulted from a technological revolution in the means of production that has necessitated more skilled and highly trained workers at the expense of unskilled labor. These changes, in turn, have led to a dramatic growth of professional, technical, "bureaucratic," and service occupations—the new working class. Although there are many disagreements over exactly which occupations should be included, there is general agreement that the criteria for inclusion as part of the (old or new) working class is that members do not own or control the means of production, and that their wages not come from direct "exploitation" of other workers. This new working class is viewed as potentially revolutionary because their working conditions allegedly generate both material exploitation and cultural opposition.[3] Ernest Mandel has offered a sharp formulation of this view:

In the framework of the third industrial revolution, manual labor is expelled from production while intellectual labor is reintroduced into the productive process on a gigantic scale. It thereby becomes to an ever-increasing degree alienated labor —standardized, mechanized, and subjected to rigid rules and regimentation, in exactly the same way that manual labor was in the first and second industrial revolutions.[4]

Post-scarcity theories, although often coupled with new working class explanations, stress the contradiction between the forces of production —which are presumed to have created the material basis for eliminating poverty and want—and the relations of production that remain structured on an assumption of scarcity. This contradiction generates both political and cultural discontent among that sector of the population that experiences post-scarcity conditions but is confronted by institutional arrangements based on the assumption of scarcity. Richard Flacks's interpretation illustrates this approach:

The root of this crisis lies in the contradiction between the technological capacities and the social organization of society. The technology frees increasing numbers from direct dependence on material production for making a living and from material insecurity. But it cannot provide either the social institutions or cultural meanings for such a post-industrial situation.[5]

In this situation, a stratum arises whose social position enables it to aspire to a life outside the goods-producing system:

This stratum contains many whose childhood and adolescent experiences lead them to feel constrained and repelled by many aspects of the prevailing culture and social order, to be extremely restless with the career opportunities for which they are programmed, and to have a considerable sense of alternative futures.[6]

In practice, the distinction between generational conflict, new working-class, and post-scarcity explanations of the New Left is seldom as sharp as I have outlined them, and Richard Flacks, in particular, uses all three in his own analysis of the New Left.

An examination of changes in the educational system, socialization process, and class structure of American society may help locate the description of the New Left activists own "conscious" creation of a theory and practice, given in previous chapters, within the context of a broader objective process of social change. This examination will not focus on psychological explanations of the New Left, but it may indicate whether or not there is a nonpsychological explanation that can account for the subjective process we have analyzed.

Education for the Millions

The importance of the university environment in shaping the New Left is acknowledged by all. The early activists themselves saw the "distorted" values found in the university as a product of the changing social role of university, while they viewed their own values as the universal and traditional values of intellectuals as a social group. Flacks, on the other hand, argues that the growth in size and concentration of universities was of critical importance in "creating" youth as a socially distinct category. Similarly, new working class theories have emphasized the changing role of knowledge and the changing functions of the university as crucial features of the changing class structure reflected in the composition of the New Left.

The recognition by the early SDS leaders that the role of the university in American society had changed was certainly valid, and it applied to the changing nature of education at all levels. In numerical terms alone, the expansion of education in the fifties and sixties was staggering. In 1930, for example, there were about 28 million elementary and secondary school pupils in the United States, and by 1950 the number had only increased to about 29 million. Between 1950 and 1968, however, the number rose to over 50 million. In percentage terms, this only represented an increase from about 90 percent of the eligible age-group to about 96 percent, but in absolute terms it placed severe strains on the financing and administering of the educational system.[7]

In college and university enrollment, the absolute increase was matched by dramatic percentage increases. For example, in 1950, the total degree-credit enrollment in colleges and universities was about 2,200,000. By 1960, the number had grown to 3,600,000 and by 1968 was over 7,000,000. In percentage terms, this amounted to an increase from 25 percent of the eligible age-group in 1950 to 38 percent in 1960, to almost 50 percent in 1968.[8]

As one might expect on the basis of these figures, the expansion of education has led to a steady increase in the over-all educational level of the American population. The median school years attained by the population (over twenty five years old) has increased from about 8½ years in 1930, to about 9½ years in 1950, to 10½ years in 1960, and by 1968 reached 12 years. Thus, by 1968, about half of the adult population had the equivalent of a high school education—perhaps not so impressive a figure when we consider that half had less than that, but nevertheless a remarkable achievement compared with other times and other societies.

What these figures do not show are the changes in the structure of the educational system that accompanied this numerical expansion. In the case of public elementary and secondary schools, for example, the sharp increase in absolute numbers has been accompanied by a proportional decrease in the number of schools, which means that the overall growth is leading to larger concentrations of students in given locations. The burden of funding elementary and secondary education has largely fallen on state and local governments, and total expenditures for this purpose have risen from about 2.2 percent of the GNP, in 1950, to about 3.8 percent in 1967-68. Aside from the increase in scale and concentration, however, elementary and secondary education has not changed radically in function.

In higher education, the changes are more fundamental. Both the size and the number of colleges and universities have increased, and in universities alone, the average enrollment increased from 8500 students, in 1950, to almost 11,000 in 1960, and between 1960 and 1964 rose to over 13,500. Between 1950 and 1964, universities increased their average enrollment by about 50 percent, while four-year liberal arts colleges and junior colleges doubled their average enrollments during the same period. The four-year liberal arts colleges and junior colleges have been growing faster than other types of institutions, and *public* junior colleges now constitute about two-thirds of all junior colleges.

Higher education also experienced changes in the pattern of financing, in part caused by a tremendous increase in the total cost of such education. In 1940, total revenue for institutions of higher education was under one billion dollars, but, by 1950, had doubled to over two billion dollars. Between 1950 and 1960, total revenue again more than doubled to almost six billion, and by 1965 reached almost 13 billion dollars. With this increase in total revenue, the sources of funding changed, with endowment earnings, private gifts, and auxilliary enterprises all remaining steady or declining as a proportion of the total. Government funding of higher education increased from about 30 percent just prior to World War II to almost 50 percent by 1944, and then fluctuated sharply between 1945 and 1956. Between 1956 and 1964, however, it again increased from about 41 percent of the total to about 47 percent.[9] While expenditures have risen steadily for all purposes, there is a relationship between types of expenditures and sources of revenue—expenditures for plant operation and maintenance and for instructional purposes rely heavily on private sources of revenue, while expenditures for research and for student aid rely heavily on government sources.[10]

These changes reflect the growing importance of education for all types of occupations, and particularly the growing need for very highly trained personnel in certain expanding categories of occupations. The development of sophisticated machines to replace unskilled human labor also generated a need for more skilled workers to operate these machines. At the same time, this change in the instruments of production caused technological progress to become ever more dependent on "scientific" progress, and the need for stronger ties between the "production" of knowledge and the production of goods increased.[11] This growing importance of knowledge in relation to technological progress led to a profound change in the role of colleges and universities, and they have been converted from a relatively insulated institution responsible for providing a "liberal" education to future leaders of society, to an institution responsible for conducting basic research and training skilled workers for business and government. This change is clearly reflected in the increased spending by universities for research, which increased from about 27 million dollars a year in 1939 to almost 734 million dollars a year in 1957.[12]

In addition to the growing importance of universities caused by technological progress, the tremendous growth of "white-collar" occupations in service industries and in federal and corporate bureaucracies also necessitated an expansion of higher education. Colleges and universities became responsible for providing the training and skills needed in business and government, and the ties between the university and other sectors of society grew more direct. In addition to increased government funding of research and student aid, for example, businesses began to recruit actively on campus. A survey by the University of Michigan placement office, in 1960, found that more than two-thirds of the companies that used its services had begun systematic recruiting only after World War II, and that over one-half had begun after 1950.[13] Kenneth Neubeck has even found indications that during the sixties some companies attempted to develop direct ties to secondary schools in order to increase the quantity and quality of trained workers for certain occupations.[14]

Thus, the function and role of education in American society has changed since World War II toward increasing interdependence between the university, business, and government, and toward an expansion of opportunities for access to higher education. The consequences of these changes are a subject of considerable debate, however. The view of early activists that the values embodied in the new university were "distorted" values quite different from the classical values of earlier times is not supported by a historical comparison of the changes in the university. The rigid organization of student life and the *in loco parentis* doctrine students found so appalling were not *new* features that resulted from changes in the university, but, on the contrary, were remnants of an earlier period when higher education was largely the province of the upper class. While the role, function, and composition of the university was changing, the values by which student life was ordered remained largely unchanged—at least initially.

In arguing that the changes in the structure of higher education were crucial in creating "youth," Flacks points to the concentration and segregation of students in a context where their privilege (draft deferments) and advantage led to both intellectual and emotional bases for social criticism and cultural opposition.[15] A similar process of concentration and segregation affected nonstudent youth, he argues, in the growth of a conscript army and in the concentration of unemployed youth in urban ghettoes. He does not explain, however, how or why these different sectors of the youth stratum could or did develop a similar social critique and a common cultural opposition. Moreover, even in his discussion of students, he seems to gloss over the class composition of the student population. The fact of the matter is that, although the social base of students did broaden during the fifties and sixties, there was considerable differential access to higher education. Private colleges and universities have expanded to allow access to the sons and daughters of those in high-paying and prestigious white-collar occupations, while public colleges and universities are available to children from lower white-collar occupations. Children of working-class parents have gained greater access to higher education, but primarily to junior colleges with limited opportunity to get a four-year college education.[16]

In addition, the specific institutional settings in which the New Left first appeared raise questions about the emphasis on generational rather than class characteristics of the New Left. James O'Brien has pointed out that the New Left first grew in the private colleges and universities and in the large state universities, and only in the late sixties began to spread to smaller campuses and to junior colleges.[17] Flacks's own studies of the social base of activists, moreover, confirm the view that, until the late sixties they were predominantly children of highly educated parents in white-collar occupations.[18]

While it is undoubtedly true that the concentration and segregation of young people in colleges and universities was an important factor in the development of a New Left, the family backgrounds of university students in general, and activists in particular, suggests that the class origins of the New Left may be more important than its generational characteristics. This possibility seems to be further strengthened by an examination of the sources of the values articulated by the New Left.

Socialization and the Family

In discussing the development of a theory and practice by the early New Left, I argued that this development represented an effort to articulate and develop a set of self-directed *values* as a basis for political action, and that the early activists saw the source of these values in characteristics of their roles as students and intellectuals. Other studies, however, have pointed out that the values articulated by the New Left represented a historically specific configuration that can be traced to changes in family socialization and child-rearing during the fifties. Richard Flacks, in particular, has emphasized the extent to which activists were socialized by their families into a value system that was at odds with the traditional Protestant, capitalist value system.[19]

In seeking a structural basis for this oppositional value system, Flacks places a great deal of emphasis on the extent to which the parents of activists were in high-paying professional occupations, and on the high educational backgrounds of both parents. From this finding, he argues that changes in the structure of capitalism *necessarily* led to changes in the middle-class family, which, in turn, "created" youths who had difficulty accepting the existing organization of society. This leads him to argue that the New Left was a political expression of an emerging stratum—an "intelligentsia"—within the educated middle class, and in attempting to explain why this oppositional value system took political form in the early sixties he adopts a post-scarcity theory of American capitalism which stresses the guilt feelings of early activists toward their special privilege. This youthful intelligentsia then becomes a "vanguard" of a distinctive youth culture, whose cultural and political opposition gradually diffuses to a broader stratum of youth through music, distinct dress, drugs, and other media.

This notion of an "intelligentsia" and the concept of the "vanguard" role of the intelligentsia (although Flacks does not fully develop this concept) seem to me extremely important to an understanding of why the New Left begins where it does, and it is consistent with my own discussion of the backgrounds and characteristics of the SDS "elite." At the same time, however, an examination of the changes that have taken place in family structure and socialization processes suggests that the values articulated by the New Left were developing among a much broader strata than is suggested by the notion of an "intelligentsia," and that the diffusion can be explained in terms of diffusion within that broader strata rather than in terms of the formation of "youth culture." It also seems to me that the emergence of this value system as an oppositional value system in the late fifties and early sixties can be explained without invoking a nebulous (and undemonstrable) theory of the "post-scarcity" character of American capitalism.

In the first place, changes in family structure and child rearing are not limited to "professionals," but have been characteristic of "middle-class" families in general. The most recognized change in family structure has been the reduction in size and the erosion of close ties beyond the unit of the nuclear family. A major cause of this change was the increasing geographic mobility of such families. In their classic community studies in the thirties, for example, Lloyd Warner and the Lynds stressed the importance of geographic stability on family and community life, and the importance of extended family units in shaping the stratification hierarchies of local communities.[20] The increasing domination of the private sector of the economy by large corporations, and the corresponding decline in family-owned small businesses, reversed this pattern. In his popular study of the life-style of the new "organization man" in the fifties, William H. Whyte observed:

The man who leaves home is not the exception in American society but the key to it. Almost by definition, the organization man is a man who left home and, as it was said of the man who went from the Midwest to Harvard, kept on going. There have always been people who left home, and the number of them is not decreasing but increasing—and so greatly that those who stay put in the home town are often as affected by the emigration as those who leave.[21]

This geographical migration is not limited to corporate life, but characterizes most of the occupations requiring high education, and studies have indicated that the higher the educational and income levels of individuals, the more likely they are to have migrated from their homes.[22] Whyte also pointed out that this high rate of migration not only made difficult the maintenance of extended families, but also imparted new qualities to community life in the "suburbias" that sprang up to house the transients.

Within the shrinking family unit, relationships were also changing during the fifties. As the size of families declined, the mother spent most of her time raising the children at home, while the father was away "at work".[23] As a consequence, children were most directly exposed to the expectations of their mothers, while their fathers became final arbiters providing a generally warm, nonauthoritarian, and supportive atmosphere.[24] Urie Bronfenbrenner described some of the changing characteristics of "middle-class" child-rearing practices during this period, and he concluded that, before World War II, these practices were more "restrictive" than those of "working-class" parents, but after the war they became more "permissive."[25] This conclusion was based on the reliance, by working-class parents, on physical discipline to control children, while middle-class parents utilized techniques that relied on the withdrawal of affection for control. He also noted, however, that toward the end of the fifties, this gap in practices narrowed, with working-class parents increasingly adopting techniques similar to those of the middle-class.

Melvin Kohn has pointed out that Bronfenbrenner's explanation of these changes (that middle-class parents read and followed "expert" advice on child-rearing) is limited in that it does not explain *why* middle-class parents read and followed that particular advice.[26] In his own study, Kohn found that working-class and middle-class parents stressed different *values* with their children; where working-class parents stressed values that emphasized conformity to external authority, middle-class parents stressed values that emphasized "self-direction" by the children. Moreover, Kohn found that these different value systems were held by the parents themselves, and that the values were related to social class:

Social class is consistently related to fathers' values for children: The higher their class position, the more highly they value self-direction and the less highly they value conformity to externally imposed standards. This is true regardless of the age and sex of the children. . . . Moreover, the relationship is much the same in all segments of the society—regardless of race, religion, national background, region of the country, and the size of the community. . . .

The higher their social class position, the more men value self-direction and the more confident they are that self-direction is both possible and efficacious. The lower their social class position, the more men value conformity and the more certain they are that conformity is all that their own capacities and the exigencies of the world allow.[27]

What makes Kohn's findings especially important in trying to understand the sources of the New Left values is that he found that the values of self-direction were not only correlated in some general way with social class, but in particular with the specific characteristics of certain occupations. Those occupations that involve complex work with data or people rather than with "things," complexly organized (routinized) tasks, and no close supervision, are most strongly related to values of self-direction. In other words, the values of self-direction depend on the extent to which a father's occupation allows and requires self-direction. Contrary to popular stereotypes of bureaucracies as places where little self-direction and creativity are allowed, Kohn found that it is precisely in bureaucratic occupations that self-directed values are fostered:

The larger the organization in which men work and the more levels of supervision it has, the more likely men are to value self-direction, to emphasize intrinsic and to de-emphasize extrinsic aspects of jobs, to hold non-authoritarian beliefs, to be receptive to innovation and change, not to be self-deprecatory, and to think that their ideas are independent of the social entities to which they belong. These relationships exist no matter whether men work in government, in profit-making firms, or in non-profit organizations. . . . Self-direction is most valued by the least closely supervised employees of large organizations; conformity is most valued by closely supervised employees of small organizations.[28]

Thus, Kohn concludes that occupation is crucial in shaping values of self-direction insofar as it determines the extent of self-direction that jobs provide or preclude. In a more recent article, Kohn and Carmi Schooler have presented additional evidence that, indeed, it is the conditions of work that shape these values, rather than selective recruitment to certain occupations of persons already holding values of self-direction.[29] Education, on the other hand, is crucial insofar as it provides or fails to provide the capability for exercising self-direction, and education and occupation together affect the *strength* of self-directed values.[30]

To summarize these findings, Kohn has found that the child-rearing *techniques* of parents reflect the *values* that parents hold for their children, that these values are also the parents' own values, that these values are shaped by the *occupation* and *education* of the parents, and that *"bureaucratic"* occupations foster values of self-direction rather than values of conformity. Carmi Schooler has done further research on the effects of this process and has found that individuals *raised* with self-directed values in a "complex, multi-faceted environment" (i.e., an environment in which the individual is called upon to make decisions on the basis of a wide variety of factors, is exposed to numerous alternative models of behavior, and can see as plausible a wide range of goals) become accustomed to having considerable freedom in determining their behavior, and as adults resist restraints and are able to cope intellectually with complex and ambiguous situations.[31]

In evaluating the significance of these changes in family socialization of children, two other considerations are important. First, these are *changes* in the *family* socialization process. What happened was that after World War II, parents, particularly those in "bureaucratic" occupations, began to adopt "self-directed" values in place of "conformist" values and stressed those new values in raising their children. During that same period, however, the educational system—also a part of the socialization process—remained structured around "conformist" values. Although the educational system grew and expanded in those years, and became more closely enmeshed with business and government, higher education still followed the *in loco parentis* doctrine, and the classroom situation remained a highly structured and disciplined environment. At the same time, more and more children were spending longer and longer portions of their lives in educational institutions. As a result of this, children raised with self-directed values by their families found themselves exposed to conformist values and expectations in their role as students.

Second, and related to this, is a certain ambivalence about the effect of these changing values. As Keniston and Flacks have pointed out, values of self-direction may help to produce independent and flexible minds, but they also may produce a sense of dislocation and discontent with existing values and institutions.[32] In the father, this may lead to an ambivalence about his job and self-worth which gets communicated to the child, while, in the mother, it may lead to a discontent with being restricted to a child-rearing role when her education has prepared her for other possibilities. This parental ambivalence can lead not only to independent and flexible children, but also to confused and discontented ones.

All of this suggests a somewhat different interpretation from that given by Flacks. The New Left began among some of the "best" students on the "best" campuses who came from families in the highest layers of the bureaucratic, white-collar strata of occupations. The strong self-directed values with which they had been reared as children conflicted with the conformist values and expectations they met as students, and their discontent led to an oppositional consciousness toward the university and other institutions. These same values were also developing throughout bureaucratic, white-collar layers, and the concentration of children from such backgrounds in colleges and universities provided a pool of students with similar values potentially open to such an oppositional consciousness.

This dichotomy between "conformist" values and "self-directed" values is somewhat similar to David Riesman's distinction between "inner-directed" and "other-directed" man,[33] but it differs significantly in that the source of the dichotomy is located in the changing class structure of American society, rather than in the character structure of individuals. Moreover, the importance of "peer group" socialization emphasized by Riesman, and by Flacks, loses some of its force as an argument for generational explanations of "youth culture" in light of the relatively homogeneous class composition both of students in general, and the New Left in particular. Thus, once again, there seems to me to be no compelling reason to turn to generational notions of "youth" as a distinct social category in order to explain the objective sources of New Left opposition.

Instead, it seems that we should turn our attention to an examination of the nature of the changes in the class structure which generated essential features of that opposition. This is necessary because only when we understand the direction and character of the economic changes that led to changes in class structure, family socialization, and education will we know how best to characterize those changes and how to evaluate the New Left that emerged out of them. Flacks, for example, has argued that these changes were necessitated by changes in the structure of capitalism, and that they *necessarily* led to an oppositional value system among some of the young. In order to evaluate this assertion, we need to know how these values related to the structure of capitalism which gave rise to them.

The Changing Class Structure

When we turn our attention to changes in the American class structure, we enter a realm of great debate on which much heat, but little light, has been shed. It is not my purpose to discuss or resolve all these debates, but merely to indicate some of the dimensions relevant to an attempt to understand the emergence of the New Left. Indeed, as I shall indicate shortly, I do not think it is possible to resolve some of the fundamental questions about the nature of the class structure with the information presently available.

In terms of its immediate political impact on the left, probably the most important characteristic of the American economy in the two decades following World War II was its almost uninterrupted growth. Between 1947 and 1969, the total gross national product more than doubled, and between 1947 and 1959 alone, it increased by 166 billion dollars. While all sectors of the economy contributed to this growth, the impact of Keynesian economics was clearly manifest in the dramatic increases in government expenditures for goods and services.[34] This continuing growth led many Americans to renewed confidence in the ability of capitalism to provide a better life and, at the same time, led the Old Left to a belief that capitalism had temporarily "stabilized" and postponed the ultimate economic crisis that seemed imminent in the thirties. Because it did not examine in depth either the forces that produced this stabilization or the long-term changes in the economy generated by this process, the Old Left became steadily more incapable of offering an analysis or strategy that was in harmony with the experiences of millions of Americans in the postwar period.

For beneath the superficial "stabilization" of American capitalism, profound changes were taking place in the organization and scale of economic life. Despite the over-all growth of the economy, for example, the pattern of growth was unevenly distributed. In terms of employment, most of the private sector either declined or remained stable as a proportion of total employment, while government workers increased from 12.5 to 17.5 percent of the total, and employment in the service sector increased from 11.5 percent to almost 16 percent.[35]

This uneven development was the result of two parallel and related processes. The first of these, as I indicated earlier, was a revolution in the instruments of production by which knowledge became more directly and immediately critical to the functioning and growth of the economy. As James O'Connor has pointed out in some detail, these changes sharply increased the overhead costs of production which formerly were met within the private sector.[36] As a result of these changes, an increasing portion of these costs began to be socialized within the public sector, costs that included the technical and scientific upgrading of the labor force; the transformation of raw labor power into technical, scientific, and administrative brain power; and scientific research and development. The state now pays for most of the costs of education and training and provides over 60 percent of research funds.[37]

Alongside this revolution in the instruments of production, and the related growth of the government sector, went a steady growth in the scale and concentration of economic power in the private sector, which necessitated a much greater emphasis on coordination and distribution functions, as opposed to direct production functions. The trend toward monopoly was well under way in the fifties, and even one as basically supportive of this trend as Adolph Berle was led to observe:

Briefly, some five hundred great corporations dominate through outright ownership two-thirds of the industry of the United States. . . . But a study of the figures on capital formation develops the fact that these same corporations accumulate the greater part of three-fifths or 60 percent of the capital which the United States applies to industrial use. This is a powerful element of control of the economic and social future of the United States. Capacity to apply that capital is capacity to determine when, where, and how future American development will go on.[38]

In a similar vein, Ferdinand Lundberg points out that in 1962 sales of five hundred largest corporations amounted to almost 42 percent of the GNP, and that these same corporations controlled more than 30 percent of the industrial assets of the nation.[39] Accompanying the growth in output, concentration, and profit of American corporations during the fifties was a decline in capacity utilization to the point that, by 1959, American industry was using only 81 percent of the capacity under use in 1950.[40]

The effect of these changes in the structure of American capitalism was a dramatic change in the occupational structure. Not only did "white-collar" and "service" occupations grow relative to "blue-collar" and "farm" occupations, but, within these broad categories, were changes that reflected the growing importance of educated and skilled labor relative to unskilled labor. In blue-collar occupations, for example, the proportion of craftsmen and foremen increased, while the proportion of operatives and nonfarm laborers declined.[41] Similarly, in white-collar occupations the proportion of "managers, officials, and proprietors" and sales-workers declined, while the proportion of clerical workers and "professional, technical, and kindred" workers sharply increased.[42] In addition to this growth of occupations requiring higher education, skills, and training, a large proportion of this growth took place in government or corporate "bureaucracies"—again a result of the increasing scale and concentration of the private sector, and the added responsibility of government to pay the costs of training and research.

What these changes illustrate, rather obviously, is a *change* in the "class structure" of American society, but it is far less obvious just how these changes should be characterized. The problem, in part, is one of definition. If, for example, we equate blue-collar occupations with "working-class" and white-collar occupations with "middle-class," then we would be inclined to say that the working-class is declining while the middle-class is growing. When we examine the changes within white-collar occupations, however, we are led to make distinctions between an "old middle class" of self-employed small entrepreneurs and a "new middle class" of salaried wage earners.[43]

If we try to go beyond such a simplistic model of the class structure (as "new working class" theories do) and attempt to bring Marxist conceptions of "ownership" and "exploitation" into the analysis, the problem becomes considerably more complicated. To develop such an analysis, it is necessary to separate the buyers of labor from the sellers of labor power, and workers whose labor is exploited from workers whose income derives—directly or indirectly—from the exploitation of others. In his excellent analysis of these problems, Donald Hodges argues that such an approach yields a model consisting of a capitalist class, a bureaucratic class, and a laboring class, with "old" and "new" segments within each of these classes.[44] The old capitalist class, he argues, consisted of the private owners and operators of their own establishments, while the new capitalist class consists of a corporate bourgeoisie, rentier, or securities-holding class; the old bureaucracy consists of public officials and managers of corporations, including all levels of supervisors, while the new bureaucracy consists primarily of specialists, technocrats, and scientific and research workers (including teachers and social workers); the old laboring class consists of the traditional "proletariat" of blue-collar and white-collar workers in industry and commerce, while the new laboring class consists of a service class of blue-collar and white-collar workers employed mainly in the public sector (including students).

Just the problem of accurately sorting workers in different occupations into these different classes presents enormous difficulties, given the kind of census data available, but the problem does not end there. Even if such a sorting out is possible, the result is a picture of the *objective* class structure, of a class structure based on common relationships to the means of production. Since the political significance of the class structure depends not only on the existence and relative size of different classes, but also on the nature and extent of "class consciousness" within different classes, we must also know something about the values, attitudes, interests, and organization that develop in these different classes. If the data necessary to develop a Marxist analysis of the objective class structure is difficult to assemble, the data necessary to describe and analyze the extent and forms of class consciousness within these classes is practically nonexistent.

Thus, even if we could resolve the conceptual and theoretical arguments implicit in the debate over "new working class" theories,[45] the lack of relevant empirical data makes it impossible, at the present time, to root an interpretation of the formation of the New Left in a *comprehensive* theory and analysis of the American class structure. Given this limitation, however, there remains one crucial observation about the nature of the objective process that fostered the development of a New Left, namely, that the changes in class structure, social relationships, and institutional structures that fostered that development were a consequence of the growth and expansion of capitalist economic organization, not its breakdown.

Thus, Flacks's argument that the structure of American capitalism necessarily generated the changes in family structure and socialization processes that led to a New Left seems valid. It is not so clear, however, that the oppositional consciousness that developed from these changes was an opposition to the new *structure* of capitalism, or whether it instead represented an opposition to older social relationships and cultural forms made obsolete by these structural changes.

The New Left in Perspective

In order to understand why the New Left emerged when it did, and its *general* significance as a social force, it is necessary to examine its development as one outcome of an objective process of social change. At the center of this process was a revolution in the mode of production that significantly altered the relationship between "knowledge" and the production of goods, and had two important consequences: first, it necessitated an upgrading of the educational and skill level of the labor force and led to a tremendous increase in the number and proportion of workers employed in public and private bureaucracies; and second, it led to an expansion of higher education and to greater interdependence between the university, on the one hand, and business and government, on the other.

These consequences contained certain contradictory elements, however. The growth of bureaucratic, white-collar occupations brought about different social relations of production (e.g., family structure) and fostered different values than those that had characterized an industrial capitalism dominated by blue-collar occupations. At the same time, these occupations were distributed throughout the economy in such a way as to inhibit the development of a shared "class consciousness" among the workers in these occupations. A large proportion were employed in federal, state, or local government bureaucracies, where formal restraints on union activity or other class-oriented organization were considerably greater than in the private sector,[46] while another inhibiting factor was the extent of geographic mobility that characterized many of these occupations.

Similarly, the changes in the mode of production led to crucial changes in the function of the university and the relationship between the university and other social institutions, but it did not lead to changes in the social relations of students within the university. Moreover, the tremendous expansion of higher education and the changing role and function of the university increased the bureaucratization and specialization of university life, which strengthened rather than weakened the "conformist" pressures on students.

As new social relations of production and self-directed values developed among highly educated workers in bureaucratic occupations, they adopted child-rearing practices that fostered these same values in their children, while the expansion of higher education concentrated ever greater numbers of children from such backgrounds in colleges and universities whose organization discouraged the expression of self-direction. The contradiction between the values and relations within the family, and those within the university, led to discontent among the children from the most advanced layers of the bureaucratic, white-collar strata, which took the form of political and cultural opposition based on self-directed values.

Thus, the objective process that generated a New Left can be viewed as a conflict between new social relations and cultural values generated by the growth, concentration, and alteration of American capitalism, and older social relations and cultural values appropriate to earlier industrial capitalism. In this sense, the New Left represented, objectively, a force for the rationalization of social relationships and cultural values *within* capitalist economic organization, rather than a force for the abolishment of that economic form. The class-related characteristics of the socialization process, composition of the student population, and composition of the New Left which reinforce such an interpretation, moreover, suggest that (at least during the early sixties) explanations that focus on generational conflict to explain the objective origins and character of the New Left cannot be adequately separated from the class factors so as to provide a satisfactory alternative explanation.

The argument that objectively the New Left represented a force for the rationalization of American capitalism may seem hard to accept in light of the increasingly anticapitalist rhetoric and "revolutionary" activity of the New Left during the late sixties. And yet, that very paradox highlights a critical issue of theory and methodology that we must turn to in concluding an examination of the development of the New Left. In order for the objective process we have discussed in this chapter to account adequately for the origins and character of the New Left in *totality*, the human beings who comprised the movement must either be viewed as passive objects whose very action was determined by the objective forces we have outlined, or as totally rational beings who understood their objective character, accepted it, and acted upon it. In fact, however, they were neither of these. As the discussion of earlier chapters indicates, the activists who comprised the New Left also *created* it, and they did so on the basis of the definitions and meanings they attached to their own experiences. The total character of the New Left can only be understood in terms of *both* the objective and the subjective processes it represented, and in an examination of the interpenetration of these two processes we may discover how the totality of the New Left both transcended, and was limited by, the objective process that shaped its general character.

7 Conclusion: The Beginning of the Decline

To those whose awareness of the New Left was shaped by the massive antiwar and student protests of the late 1960s, it may seem more than a little "academic" to devote so much attention to the development of a New Left theory and practice during the period leading up to 1966. And it is certainly true that for a full understanding of the character of the New Left during the years of its greatest influence, it will be necessary to investigate other processes than those discussed in these pages. The changing relations between the New Left and the government (which was no longer "liberal" after 1968); relations within and between the black, women's, antiwar, and student movements of the late sixties; and the changing economic relations that characterized American society—all of these must be examined in detail and in connection with the relations that comprised the New Left in its formative years before a fuller understanding is possible.

Implicit in the approach I have followed, however, is a belief that the character and significance of the New Left after 1966 can only be understood as an outgrowth of the process of formation prior to that period —indeed, that the sources of both the growth and the disintegration of the organized New Left in later years can be found within that process of formation. I began this account by criticizing the tendency of some earlier studies of the New Left to treat it as a social movement that was largely *determined* by psychological or social-structural factors outside the control of the activists who comprised the movement. My own approach, in contrast, has been to treat the development of the New Left as a creative activity by those who comprised it, and to explore the interconnection within and between its character as a conscious product of the participants and its character as a manifestation of structural changes in American society.

For purposes of presentation, I have separated the analysis of these two processes, but I do not mean to imply that they were isolated or autonomous in their actual development. In order to bring these relationships back into perspective and to outline some of the connections between the character of the New Left in the late sixties and the processes that shaped it during its formative years, I want to briefly sketch the development of the New Left after 1966.

Resistance and Revolution

While the early SDS activists asserted from the beginning their aim of building a *new* left, in the late sixties many argued that the movement should just be *the* left. This indicates more about the subjective differences between early and later activists than it does about the actual difference between the "reformist" and "revolutionary" New Left. By the end of 1965, the efforts of the initial SDS elite to develop a theory and practice based on their self-directed values had largely ended in failure. Anarchist and voluntarist ideas prevented the development of any kind of a theoretical "line" for SDS and, at the same time, insured that political and organizational experience were not passed on to new recruits. The closest thing to such a line—the strategy of building an interracial movement of the poor—was already in question with the failure of the ERAP projects to gain a firm rooting in local communities. An earlier decision to create an adult wing of the SDS had not been carried out, and the decision not to take the leadership of the burgeoning antiwar movement insured the further isolation of the organization from key political struggles.

Events, however, did not wait for the SDS to solve its internal problems. The war in Vietnam continued to escalate, while opposition to the war mounted; after the rebuff of the Mississippi Freedom Democratic party, at the 1964 Democratic convention, the black movement began to turn away from an alliance with white liberals toward a separatist position; and struggles for university reform continued to spread. All of these led to an escalation and expansion of political activity, but also to the organizational fragmentation of that activity. Where, earlier, SDS had been the umbrella organization with a multi-issue focus that tried to give all left activists a sense of belonging to the same movement, now a series of single-issue movements appeared, often with rather different politics and constituencies. The decision of SNCC to exclude whites, and the later emergence of the Black Panthers, firmly separated the black and white movements and forced the whites to seek their own issues and organizations. The barbarism of the Vietnam war and the threat of the draft led to a huge increase in the numbers protesting that war, but the refusal of SDS to guide that protest allowed the Old Left and pacifist organizations to reemerge as a significant political force, and by 1966 they had established the first of what turned out to be a series of national coalitions to lead the antiwar movement: the National Coordinating Committee Against the War in Vietnam. This was later followed successively by the Spring Mobilization Committee Against the War, the National Mobilization Committee Against the War, the New Mobilization Committee Against the War, and this group later split, with the Communists, socialists, pacifists, and religious groups forming the People's Coalition for Peace and Justice, while the Trotskyists formed the National Peace Action Coalition.

Meanwhile, the university reform protests led to a separate student movement, which tended to support antiwar protest and the black movement, but was organizationally separate. It was only in the last that SDS remained a guiding force, and through the student campaigns its membership continued to grow.

The effect of all these developments was somewhat ambiguous. On the one hand, they produced a numerical growth of the left (old and new) unparalleled since the thirties. They also helped to impart a sense of crisis, as time went on, about the general condition of the American system, and spurred debate about the need for fundamental changes. At the same time, however, the fragmented character of these developments led to piecemeal and competing strategies for organizing.

The intensification of all these struggles—but particularly the antiwar struggle—led to a shift in tactics, as *protest* against government policies escalated into *resistance* to those policies—and talk of the need for revolution in America began to spread. The search by the New Left for a revolutionary strategy led, ironically, back to Marxism. As Carl Oglesby put it in 1969: "The necessity of a revolutionary strategy was, in effect, the same thing as the necessity of Marxism-Leninism. There was—and is—no other coherent, integrative, and explicit philosophy of revolution."[1]

The years of 1968 and 1969 saw a return to the disputes of the Old Left. We must organize workers! We must organize the "new working class"! We must organize youth! We must create a vanguard party! We must create a united front! It was a time when the young activists of the sixties returned to their revolutionary ancestors, and if they accepted too uncritically what they found there, it must be said that little in their experience had prepared them for the task that confronted them. For the SDS, in particular, this was the time when new working class theories were given serious consideration. Faced with the "middle-class" backgrounds of most whites in the movement, the activists found it difficult to accept a traditional Marxist division between bourgeoisie and proletarians, without altering the definition of the proletariat. In a major speech in 1967, Greg Calvert, one of the SDS leaders, outlined a new SDS theoretical stance:

What we have come to understand is that the great American middle class is not middle class at all. None of the 19th century definitions of the bourgeoisie apply: not the upper bourgeoisie—the owners of capital; not the petty bourgeoisie—the owners of small property; not, finally, even the professional bourgeoisie. . . . The vast majority of those whom we call middle class must properly be understood as members of the "new working class", that is, as the workers who fill the jobs created by a new level of technological development within the same exploitative system. . . . Students are the "trainees" for the new working class and the factory-like multiversities are the institutions which prepare them for their slots in the bureaucratic machinery of corporate capitalism. . . . Students are in fact a key group in the creation of the productive forces of this super-technological capitalism.[2]

This analysis provided temporary ideological relief in the late sixties and was a theoretical basis for SDS student organizing throughout 1968, but in the fragmented context of the times it was vulnerable to attack in two ways: first, it was openly "elitist" and justified ignoring the real oppression of blacks, poor people, and workers; and second, while accepting the Marxist-Leninist notion that only workers could make the revolution, it performed a twist of logic by calling anyone who made the revolution a worker.

With the acceptance of Marxist categories of analysis by the New Left, the door was opened for an ideological assault from a reinvigorated Old Left, and the attack came in full force from the Progressive Labor party and the Young Socialist Alliance—the "Maoists" and the "Trots." PL ridiculed the new working class analysis and called upon students to give up any pretense of being a revolutionary force themselves. It urged students to organize workers "at the point of production" and to help build a vanguard party of true proletarians, and it argued that the oppression of blacks, women, and similar groupings was secondary to class oppression.[3] In its insistence on doctrinal purity, PL treated all forms of nationalism as counterrevolutionary, and went so far as to criticize the Vietnamese for entering peace talks with the United States, calling instead for a military victory over imperialism.

From another direction, the YSA criticized SDS for concentrating on local organizing rather than mass demonstrations, and for not treating the war as the central issue around which to build a united front of workers, students, and professionals. Arguing for the "least common denominator," the YSA urged that militant direct action be subordinated to peaceful protest that could attract large numbers, and that would lead to a spread of socialist ideas. In organizational terms, however, where PL decided to enter and try to win over control of SDS, the YSA chose to enter and try to take over a student antiwar organization, the Student Mobilization Committee.

Under attack on several fronts from the Old Left, new working class theorizing gave way to an attempt to develop an analysis that would merge students with other oppressed groups, and during 1969 the notion of a Revolutionary Youth Movement of students and white working-class youth was developed. At the SDS convention that year, the different positions met head on and split the organization, with the Weathermen emerging as the chief carriers of the RYM position. Briefly, the Weathermen argued that the nation-state is dead, having given way to the empire. The industrial democracies of NATO form the world bourgeoisie of the new system, and the colonial and neocolonial states of the third world constitute the world proletariat. The task of white radicals in the "mother country" was to create a "white fighting force" of working-class youth to disrupt the empire from within, but the black and third world liberation movements constitute the true vanguard of the revolution.[4]

A year later, the Weathermen had gone underground to direct a campaign of bombing and guerilla warfare, and within two years the national organizations of the New Left had almost all dissolved. In their place, however, were new formations of "communes" and "collectives" at the local level which, although not always "political" in the sense that was common during most of the sixties, still were seen as part of the same "movement" of opposition to existing structures.

The Separation of Culture and Politics

Throughout the early sixties, "political" opposition and "cultural" opposition had developed side by side. The revival of political protest was accompanied by a folk music revival and the spread of "coffeehouse culture," and many of the political activists were involved in these as well as in political activity. The civil-rights movement not only provided a testing ground for political ideas and practice, but in the "Freedom Houses" where activists lived and worked together, efforts to develop "communal" life-styles and experimentation with sexual relationships and mores became an important aspect of becoming a radical. Music played a crucial role in forging emotional bonds and feelings of solidarity in the southern campaigns, as well as a way of spreading the message to others. In the SDS, as well, issues of "style" were crucial, and as time passed radicals adopted hair styles and manners of dress and speaking that served to provide visible and distinctive features that set them apart from those they opposed.

In the late sixties, however, the cultural and political aspects of New Left opposition began to develop along separate paths. Experiments with communal living and sex, while remaining as aspects of political activity, also were adapted to "nonpolitical" uses, the well publicized "hippies" being only the most visible of these efforts. Religious cults emphasizing communal living and personal salvation, "encounter groups" and other "sensitivity training" techniques, and a "drug and rock" culture—all grew and spread as visible manifestations of a "cultural" opposition to features of American life that was not, overtly, a political opposition. "Underground" newspapers, which in the early years tended to focus on political analysis and propaganda, began to change as well, and new papers concentrating primarily on drugs, sex, and music grew up alongside of, or in place of, papers focusing on political activity. There even developed two separate "news services" for underground papers: the Liberation News Service, which was predominantly "political," and the Underground Press Syndicate, which was predominantly "cultural."

In addition to this separation of cultural opposition from political opposition, cultural issues began to be raised as political issues—and resulted in new movements of protest. Ever since the early days of ERAP and the Mississippi Summer Project, relations between men and women within the movement had been a source of tension and discussion, as women wondered why—in a struggle directed against social inequality and manipulation—they should always be subordinate to male leadership and perform the most menial tasks. As early as the 1967 SDS convention, this concern led to a resolution on the role of women in the movement, and at various SDS meetings during the previous year women often met in separate workshops to discuss their role.[5] By the early seventies, these concerns had mushroomed into a full-blown "women's movement" with separate organizations, issues, and as many internal splits as the black movement, the Old Left, and the New Left.

Within the black movement, too, the process of radicalization led not only to separatist political organizing with an anticapitalist focus, but also to separatist "cultural" organizing, often with a procapitalist focus. The wearing of "Afro" hair styles, African dress, the taking of African names, these and other cultural expressions of "black is beautiful" gained popularity, and often fostered self-help programs and "black capitalism" as counterstrategies to the revolutionary programs of SNCC or the Black Panthers. As cultural nationalism spread in black communities, cultural differences often became a focus for political organizing and provided symbols of opposition, if not the structural reality of change. (It seems interesting that the growth of cultural nationalism really spread *after* the ghetto rebellions of 1964-68, and it may, in part, reflect an alternative to the kind of armed conflict that brought forth major reprisals.)

The separation of cultural and political opposition to the American system not only further fragmented the organizational structure of opposition, but also isolated into separate spheres the two elements whose combination in the early sixties had imparted to the New Left a significance beyond that implied in the structural process that generated it. Some sense of the profound effect of this separation on the political New Left is reflected in an important article analyzing the growing problems, written in 1969:

For in the last analysis sectarianism, dogmatism, and rhetoric are merely the most obvious signs that a movement . . . has begun to lose its momentum, has begun to turn in upon itself, has begun to place more importance on how it talks to itself than on how it talks to the people. . . .

The things that in a very immediate sense brought us to the movement—the comradeship of total, collective, active opposition to the system we hated and the glimpses of what an alternative way of life could be like—came to appear as so many forms of liberal self-indulgence as compared to the Real Needs of the People.[6]

The New Left as a Social Force

Although this brief sketch of developments after 1966 is extraordinarily superficial, it does, I think, accurately depict the central features of the political direction of the New Left during those years: the increasingly "revolutionary" self-image of activists, the revival of Old Left theory and practice, the organizational fragmentation, and the separation of cultural and political opposition. All of these, it seems to me, can be traced to the failure of the New Left during its formative years to resolve the contradiction between its role in the historical process of structural change that brought it into being, and its subjective identity as a force for the fundamental redistribution of political and economic power.

The origins of the New Left can be traced to profound changes in the structure of American capitalism. These changes altered the relationship between the production of knowledge and the production of goods and necessitated widespread changes in class structure and in the function of, and relations between, different social institutions. As a result of these changes, "bureaucratic" and other white-collar occupations , grew in both size and importance, and the university gained a critical importance, both as a source of scientific and technical knowledge and as the place where the training and skills necessary in these occupations were imparted to future workers. At the same time, unskilled labor became more marginal to the productive process, while the owners of capital and industry became more dependent on the bureaucratic and technical workers who managed the economy.

These changes in the social relations of production were not immediately accompanied by changes in the institutionalized relationships among groups, however, nor were they accompanied by changes in the "cultural" organization of institutions to reflect the values, beliefs, and interests of a growing stratum of highly educated and skilled workers. What the New Left represented, objectively, in this historical process was an attempt to *rationalize* institutional relationships and cultural organization, to bring them in line with the changes in the social relations of production. The attempt to develop a political theory and practice based on the "self-directed'' values of this strata was aimed, in this sense, at institutionalizing those values, interests, and beliefs fostered by the working conditions of educated white-collar workers.

In the subjective development of New Left theory and practice, however, this rationalizing character went unrecognized. The attempt to articulate these values by the early activists reflected their backgrounds in the most highly educated and most privileged sectors of the expanding strata, insofar as they distinguished themselves both from capitalists and from the traditional proletariat, but they confused their own opposition and values with the opposition and values of the most marginal strata of the labor force—blacks and "the poor." In placing institutionalized power and bureaucracy as the main *obstacles* to self-directed values, they confused the desire to rationalize social relationships *within* a system of structured social inequality with a desire to abolish social inequality—indeed, with the abolishing of the very structures that gave rise to their values.

The consequences of this contradiction between the objective and subjective identity of the New Left were both complex and far-reaching. During the early development of the New Left, what the SDS people *did* as a result of their subjective identity was compatible with the expression and institutionalization of self-directed values. At the same time, however, the lack of what I have called an "historical self-consciousness" on the part of the young activists led both to the breakdown and abandonment of any theoretical coherence in SDS and also toward the fragmentation and paralysis of SDS as an organization, a process that led to the disintegration of the early elite as a cohesive leadership group in the organization.

During the early sixties, it is probably fair to say that all significant political protest by the left was either directed by the New Left theory and practice or by the black movement, whose practice in those years was compatible with the values of the New Left. After 1966, however, a very different pattern emerged. Major sections of the black movement excluded whites from participation and adopted disciplined and rigid organizational forms incompatible with the expression of self-directed values. The antiwar movement was led by Old Left organizations who not only opposed the theory and practice that characterized the early New Left, but who also were not moved by the same values that moved the new activists.

Only the student movement remained a direct expression of New Left activity, but in trying to develop a new and "revolutionary" theory and practice for the late sixties, it faced very different conditions than the SDS of the early years. For the first time, the objective and subjective identities of the New Left came into serious conflict with one another, as the revolutionary trajectory of the black movement with which they identified set an example of disciplined and hierarchical organization that ran counter to the informal and flexible style set in the early New Left. Moreover, although the SDS for the first time attempted to come to grips with its historical identity in the experiment with new working class theories in 1967 and 1968, both the strengthened position of the Old Left resulting from the antiwar movement and the deep-rooted "antielitism" resulting from its own earlier theory and practice made untenable the adoption of such a theoretical stance in the later period.

These special conditions posed a difficult choice to the activists of the late sixties: either to accept the logic of their subjective identification with a revolutionary movement aimed at overturning the racial and class-based structure of power and privilege in American society, and in the process abandon the self-directed values that had guided and shaped their political activity; or to continue to develop and act upon those values, but in the process abandon political activity that inhibited the expression of those values. Both options were followed, and while many "dropped out" to become part of an increasingly apolitical "counterculture," others sought to renounce their "white skin privilege" by joining PL, YSA, or other Marxist sects. The Revolutionary Youth Movement strategy represented a brief attempt to keep revolutionary political activity united with a cultural opposition rooted in self-directed values, but its end product of Weatherman ended up as a total rejection of the objective origins of the New Left.

Thus, in a curious way, the very lack of an historical self-consciousness that led to the internal contradictions and eventual disintegration of the New Left also led to its most important contributions to the rebuilding of an American left. Because the early SDS activists did not recognize their objective character as a force for the rationalization of social relationships within an expanding and changing capitalist system, but, instead, identified their opposition with forces objectively opposed to the structure of that system, they gave greater visibility and strength to those forces. In their role as an *oppositional* force—regardless of the nature of that oppostion —they shattered the political quiescence that had characterized the fifties and challenged the view that ideology was dead and capitalism effectively stabilized. Moreover—in part because they treated opposition to existing social relationships as the primary criteria for inclusion in a New Left, and in part because they lacked any strong identification with a particular tradition of left opposition—they refused to apply narrow standards of political "correctness" as conditions for inclusion in that New Left, and, in so doing, they gradually forced a reversal of the exclusionary practice that characterized the left in the fifties.

In all of these relations within and between subjective and objective processes of development, the character and significance of the New Left as a social force were shaped. Viewed in one way, the New Left contributed significantly to the rebuilding of an American left and projected visible alternative models of living and working together. Viewed from another standpoint, the New Left was but a manifestation of an expanding and changing capitalist system, whose theory and practice served to obscure the true nature of that system and to postpone its downfall. Such evaluations, however, only underscore the fact that the New Left was comprised of real men and women *in their social relations*. The task of social science is not to judge the men and women, but to describe the sources, connections, and consequences of the relations in which they were enmeshed. Judgment takes place within those relations as they are lived. In closing this brief account of the New Left's formative years, however, it seems appropriate to briefly speculate on its long-term significance.

The New Left and the Future

The early SDS leaders were among the "best" students at the "best" colleges and universities. To the extent that information is available, it appears that, on the whole, their parents were highly educated and employed in high-level positions in government bureaucracies or professions. In the late sixties, however, protest spread to smaller colleges and universities, and the social composition of activists broadened to include students whose families were located in lower-level positions in the bureaucracies and lower-level white-collar occupations.[7] While the self-directed value system underlying New Left opposition was generated by conditions affecting these occupations as a whole, there is evidence that the strength of these values varies with education and with the size of, and position within, these occupations. Moreover, it is not at all clear that the entire strata of white-collar occupations are part of a single social class. Hodges, for example, would argue that a minority of high-level occupations are part of an expanding "bureaucratic" class, while the vast majority are part of the "laboring" class.[8] If, indeed, large sections of the expanding white-collar occupations are being "proletarianized," then their potential as a revolutionary political force may be quite different from that of the early New Left. Without a great deal more empirical data than now exists about the nature of different white-collar occupations, however, this remains pure speculation.

The role and function of the university, too, has undergone some changes since the early sixties. As the growth and expansion of the American economy slowed in the late sixties, the "production" of trained workers by the universities caught up with the demand, and there is now a surplus of overeducated workers unable to find employment commensurate with their skills.[9] Indeed, in certain respects, the university now acts as a labor reservoir that helps hold down the unemployment rate. The effects of this change are also difficult to evaluate and probably depend in part on whether it represents a short-term phenomenon. It is not unreasonable to speculate, however, that it may act as a further proletarianizing influence on educated white-collar workers, removing the privileges and status that possession of skills in scarce supply bestows upon the possessor.

The early New Left was a rationalizing force both because it was drawn from the most privileged sections of the strata being generated by the development of American capitalism and because the character of that development bestowed a privileged position on the possessors of the skills required in these strata. The early New Left was an oppositional force because that process of rationalization required changes in the social relationships and cultural organization that characterized certain institutions at the time. To the extent that the New Left met strong opposition to the changes required by their self-directed values, the *political* character of New Left opposition broadened and became more radical. To the extent that institutions changed and adapted to accommodate these self-directed values, the political character of New Left opposition lessened and narrowed to a cultural opposition.

Whether these changes in the structural features of American society that gave rise to a New Left in the early sixties represent a long-term trend that may merge the objective characteristics of the movement with its original subjective identity is, of course, an issue beyond the scope of the present study. Whatever the future characteristics and strength of the American left, it will probably look quite different from the New Left of the sixties. And yet, just as the formation and development of the New Left can only be understood in relation to the experiences of an earlier left, the future of radical politics in America cannot help but be shaped by the experiences of the New Left. I hope that this study contributes to an understanding of that experience.

Notes

Introduction

1. Michael W. Miles, *The Radical Probe* (New York: Atheneum, 1971), pp. 3-4.

2. An excellent collection of "movement" analyses is found in Massimo Teodori, *The New Left: A Documentary History* (New York: Bobbs-Merrill, 1969).

3. Lewis S. Feuer, *The Conflict of Generations* (New York: Basic Books, 1968), p. 530.

4. Ibid., p. viii.

5. Kenneth Keniston, *Young Radicals* (New York: Harcourt, Brace & World, 1968), p. 260.

6. Richard Flacks, "The Liberated Generation: An Exploration of the Roots of Student Protest," in *Journal of Social Issues* 23 (1967): 52-75. Also see, Julian Foster and Durward Long, *Protest! Student Activism in America* (New York: William Morrow & Co., 1970).

7. Lewis Feuer, p. 11.

8. Ibid., p. 25.

9. Ibid., p. 531.

10. Richard Flacks, "Revolt of the Young Intelligentsia," in *The New American Revolution,* eds. Roderick Aya and Norman Miller (New York: The Free Press, 1971), p. 223.

11. James O'Brien, "Beyond Reminiscence: The New Left in History," in *Radical America* 6, no.4 (July-August 1972): 12.

12. Ibid.

13. C. Wright Mills, *The Sociological Imagination* (London: Oxford University Press, 1959), p. 4.

14. Karl Marx, *The Eighteenth Brumaire of Louis Bonaparte* (Moscow: Progress Publishers, 1972), p. 10.

15. See Lewis M. Killian, "Social Movements," in *Handbook of Modern Sociology,* ed. Robert E. L. Faris (Chicago: Rand McNally & Co., 1964), p. 427.

16. See, for example, E. P. Thompson, *The Making of the English Working Class* (New York: Vintage Books, 1963).

17. Bertell Ollman, *Alienation: Marx's Conception of Man in Capitalist Society* (Cambridge: Cambridge University Press, 1971), p. 17.

18. Ibid., p. 16.

Chapter 1
The End of "The End of Ideology"

1. SDS, *Constitution,* June 1962 (SDS Collection, Tamiment Library of New York University). (Mimeographed.) Hereafter this collection is cited as Tamiment Library SDS collection.

2. SDS, *Port Huron Statement,* June 1962 (Students for a Democratic Society Papers, in the State Historical Society of Wisconsin). (Mimeographed.) Hereafter this collection is cited as SDS Papers, in the State Historical Society of Wisconsin.

3. U.S. Congress, House, Committee on Internal Security, *Anatomy of a Revolutionary Movement: Students for a Democratic Society,* HR 91-1565 (Washington: U.S. Government Printing Office, 1970), p. 3.

4. SDS, *Port Huron Statement,* p. 52.

5. Karin Ashley, et al., "You Don't Need a Weatherman to Know Which Way the Wind Blows," resolution passed at 1969 SDS Convention, reprinted in *Weatherman,* ed. Harold Jacobs (California: Ramparts Press, 1970), p. 53.

6. For an excellent history of these struggles, see John Hope Franklin, *From Slavery to Freedom* (New York: Vintage Books, 1969).

7. For an excellent discussion of competing ideological themes in the history of black political activity, see Harold Cruse, *The Crisis of the Negro Intellectual* (New York: William Morrow & Co., 1967).

8. Martin Luther King, Jr., *Stride Toward Freedom* (New York: Perennial Library, 1964), p. 94.

9. These figures are reported by Howard Zinn in his account of the sit-in movement, *SNCC: The New Abolitionists* (Boston: Beacon Press, 1964).

10. For a good description of local campaigns, see James Peck, *Freedom Ride* (New York: Grove Press, 1962). An excellent analysis of the development of the sit-ins is Anne Braden, "The Southern Freedom Movement in Perspective," *Monthly Review* 17, no. 3 (July-August 1965).

11. See, for example, Anne Braden. This description is also based on my interviews with former SNCC leaders.

12. Frantz Fanon, *The Wretched of the Earth* (New York: Grove Press, 1963). For a sociological discussion of the applicability of this model to black Americans, see Robert Blauner, *Racial Oppression in America* (New York: Harper & Row, 1972).

13. Anne Braden.

14. SNCC, *Statement of Purpose,* reprinted in Massimo Teodori, *The*

New Left: A Documentary History (New York: Bobbs-Merrill, 1969), p. 99.

15. This conference is reported in Anne Braden.

16. Memo from Tom Hayden to Al Haber, "Memo to Haber on SNCC meeting, Jackson, Miss., Sept. 14-17, 1961," (Tamiment Library SDS collection).

17. This change is reported in Howard Zinn.

18. The notion that political activity based on radical ideology had come to an end was widespread among the "left" intellectuals of the fifties. See, for example, Daniel Bell, *The End of Ideology* (New York: The Free Press, 1960).

19. Letter to the National Office of the Student League of Industrial Democracy, March 1, 1959 (Tamiment Library SDS collection). The Wisconsin Liberal Club was a SLID chapter.

20. The reasons why Old Left organizations were unable to take advantage of this interest are discussed in the next chapter.

21. Letter to the National Office of the Student League for Industrial Democracy, April 3, 1967 (Tamiment Library SLID collection).

22. See Paul Jacobs and Saul Landau (eds.), *The New Radicals*, (New York: Vintage Books, 1966), p. 94.

23. SLATE, "On the University," *Cal Reporter*, March 1958. Reprinted in Jacobs and Landau, p. 95.

24. Mike Miller and Jerry Greenberg, "SLATE Summer Conference," *The Liberal Democrat*, September 1961, p. 11.

25. For a good sampling of these debates, see *Arms and Foreign Policy in the Nuclear Age*, ed. Milton Rakove (Chicago: American Foundation for Continuing Education, 1964).

26. See Massimo Teodori, *The New Left: A Documentary History* (New York: Bobbs-Merrill), p. 23-24.

27. The main source of information on Student SANE comes from internal memos of other student organizations at the time—particularly the Young People's Socialist League, Student Peace Union and National Student Association. See, for example, letter from Michael Parker to Tom Barton, 9 December 1960 (Tamiment Library YPSL collection).

Chapter 2
Dissent in the Fifties

1. A good account of the development of foreign policy is, George F.

Kennan, *American Diplomacy 1900-1950* (Chicago: University of Chicago Press, 1951). For some sense of how the political climate affected dissent, see I.F. Stone, *The Haunted Fifties* (New York: Vintage Books, 1963).

2. I am here touching only on the political activities of labor. For a more complete discussion of the development of the labor movement, Philip Taft presents a view sympathetic to the anti-Communist position in *Organized Labor in American History* (New York: Harper & Row, 1964). There is no similar comprehensive history from a left perspective, although there are some good partial accounts. See, for example, Ronald Radosh, *American Labor and U.S. Foreign Policy: The Cold War in the Unions from Gompers to Lovestone* (New York: Vintage Books, 1970); Art Preis, *Labor's Giant Step* (New York: Pathfinder Press, 1964). The issues of *Labor History* also provide many detailed accounts of the growth of the labor movement.

3. Leo Troy, "Trade Union Membership, 1897-1962," in *The Review of Economics and Statistics*, February 1965, pp. 93-94.

4. C. Wright Mills, *White Collar* (London: Oxford University Press, 1951).

5. U.S. Department of Commerce, Bureau of the Census, *Statistical Abstract of the United States*, (Washington: Government Printing Office, 1971), table 347, p. 222.

6. U.S. Department of Labor, *Manpower Report of the President—1972*, (Washington: Government Printing Office, 1972), table C-5, p. 269.

7. Cited in Martin Oppenheimer, "What is the New Working Class?" in *New Politics* 10, (Fall 1972).

8. Among these were several large unions, including the United Electrical, Radio and Machine Workers of America, the Transport Workers Union, the Furniture Workers, and the International Longshoremen's and Warehousemen's Union—as well as other smaller unions. Most of these either gave in to the anti-Communist purge or declined in strength as a result of "raiding" by unions headed by anticommunists. See Philip Taft for a more detailed description.

9. See U.S. Congress, House, Committee on Un-American Activities, *Hearings Regarding Communist Infiltration of Labor Unions*, 81st Congress, 1st session, part I (Washington: Government Printing Office, 1949), p. 240.

10. Philip Taft, p. 571.

11. This was a recurrent theme in novels and articles of the time. For an account of the treatment of this theme by writers, see Daniel Aaron, *Writers on the Left* (New York: Harcourt, Brace, & World, 1961).

12. Gilbert Green discussed this in *The Enemy Forgotten* (New York: International Publishers, 1956).

13. See, for example, Theodore Draper, *The Roots of American Communism* (New York: Viking Press, 1957); and *American Communism and Soviet Russia* (New York: Viking Press, 1960). See also Daniel Aaron.

14. Arthur Schlesinger, Jr., *The Vital Center* (New York: Houghton Mifflin Co., 1949), p. 2.

15. A very good retrospective account of the competition between the Communists and Socialists during the thirties is *As We Saw the Thirties*, ed. Rita James Simon (Urbana: University of Illinois Press, 1967).

16. Norman Thomas, *A Socialist's Faith* (New York: W.W. Norton Co., 1951), p. 221.

17. See, for example, the *Socialist Call*, 7 July 1950.

18. For a detailed list of these splits, and bibliography on the various sects, see *Bulletin of the Tamiment Library*, no. 47, April 1971 (New York University Libraries).

19. See, for example, the resolution on the "Russian" question adopted by the SWP in December 1937 (Tamiment Library SWP collection). (Mimeographed.)

20. Young Socialists, *Handbook*, undated in early fifties (Tamiment Library YPSL Collection). (Mimeographed.)

21. Christopher Lasch, "The Cultural Cold War," in *The Agony of the American Left* (New York: Vintage Books, 1966), pp. 63-114.

22. See, for example, A.J. Muste, "What is Left to Do?" in *Fellowship*, July 1951.

23. Interview with David McReynolds, 14 December 1971.

24. The dissolution of the LYL was reported in the *National Guardian*, 11 March 1957.

25. Labor Youth League, "Statement of Principles," November 1950 (Tamiment Library LYL Collection). (Mimeographed.)

26. Ibid.

27. U.S. Department of Labor, "Employment Status of Young Workers 16 to 24 Years Old: Annual Averages, 1947-69," table A-6, in *Manpower Report of the President, 1972* (Washington: Government Printing Office, 1972).

28. Interview with Richard Ward, 28 July 1972.

29. See, for example, Hyman Lumer, "On Party Youth Work," in *Political Affairs*, June 1959.

30. See, for example, Andre Schiffrin, "The Student Movement in the 1950s: A Reminiscence," in *Radical America* 2, no. 3, (May-June 1968).

31. Ibid., p. 26.

32. For an account of YPSL in the thirties, see Hal Draper, "The Student Movement of the Thirties: A Political History," in *As We Saw The Thirties*, ed. Rita James Simon.

33. YPSL, "National Organizational Committee Minutes," 20 August 1953 (Tamiment Library YPSL Collection). (Mimeographed.)

34. Named after Max Schachtman, leader of the ISL.

35. Interview with David McReynolds, 14 December 1971.

36. Young Socialist League National Action Committee, "Draft Resolution on Socialist Realignment and Socialist Unity," 6 January 1957. (Mimeographed document in author's personal collection.)

37. Interview with David McReynolds, 14 December 1971.

38. See "Proceedings, 1960 National Convention, SP-DSF," in *New America*, 21 September 1960.

39. James O'Brien estimates that the Young Socialist tendency represented about one quarter of the YSL. See James P. O'Brien, "The Development of a New Left in the United States, 1960-1965," unpublished Ph.D. dissertation (Department of History, University of Wisconsin, 1971). For an account of the group that later became the YSA, see the *Young Socialist,* January 1959. The May-June 1958 issue of the same paper lists Young Socialist Clubs in New York, Philadelphia, Yellow Springs, Detroit, Chicago, Madison, Denver, Los Angeles, the Bay Area, Portland, and Seattle.

40. James P. O'Brien.

41. See James Weinstein, *The Decline of Socialism in America: 1912-1925* (New York: Monthly Review Press, 1967), especially pp. 84-93. Weinstein also provides one of the best accounts of the American left before the Bolshevik Revolution, and the initial split between the Communists and Socialists.

42. Interview with David McReynolds, 14 December 1971.

43. See, for example, "The Class of '49," in *Fortune*, June 1949; "The Younger Generation," in *Time*, 5 November 1951; "A Generation of Esthetes?" in *Life*, 26 November 1951; "The Careful Young Men," Symposium in the *Nation*, 9 March 1957.

44. Rose K. Goldsen, *What College Students Think* (New York: D. Van Nostrand, 1960), p. 212.

45. Philip E. Jacob, *Changing Values in College: An Exploratory Study of the Impact of College Teaching* (Evanston: Harper & Row, 1957).

46. See Kalman Siegel, "College Freedoms Being Stifled by Students' Fear of Red Label," *New York Times*, 10 May 1951.

47. Philip E. Jacob, p. 32.

48. Rose K. Goldsen, p. 223.

49. Penn Kimball, "The 'Terribly Normal' Classes of '52," *New York Times Magazine*, 8 June 1952, pp. 14-15.

50. For an account of the formation of the NSA, see William B. Welsh, "United States National Student Association," in *Higher Education*, 1 November 1948.

51. See, for example, Eugene Schwartz and Robert West, "The World Student Congress and International Education of American Students," in *Higher Education*, 15 March 1951.

52. For a discussion of the CIA role, see Sol Stern, "NSA and the CIA," in *Ramparts,* March 1967. Also see *New York Times*, 14-16 February 1967.

53. The NSA received a grant of $128,000 from the Ford Foundation to bring foreign students to the U.S., reported in "Grant for Student Leadership," *Higher Education,* December 1955. The Algerian matter was reported in *New York Times*, 15 February 1967.

54. William T. Dentzler, "Programs for International Understanding: Student Activities," in *Educational Record*, October 1952, p. 556.

55. NSA, *Student Government Bulletin*, February 1956, p. 10.

56. Among the most notable works of the Beat genre were: Allan Ginsberg, *Howl* (San Francisco: City Light Books, 1956); Jack Kerouac, *On The Road* (New York: New American Library, 1958) and *The Dharma Bums* (New York: New American Library, 1958); and Lawrence Ferlingetti, *A Coney Island of the Mind* (San Francisco: City Light Books, 1958).

57. The best description of the Beat movement is Lawrence Lipton's *The Holy Barbarians* (New York: Julian Mesner, 1959). For an interesting discussion of the Beat influence on the development of a New Left, see Jack Newfield, *A Prophetic Minority* (New York: New American Library, 1966). His book remains one of the best accounts of the early years of the New Left.

Chapter 3
No Tests East or West

1. These data are taken from officers' reports, financial reports, and organizational records of the Student Peace Union available in the Student Peace Union Papers, in the State Historical Society of Wisconsin. All data in this chapter are based on this material unless otherwise indicated.

2. SPU, *Constitution*, adopted 31 October 1959 (SPU Papers, in the State Historical Society of Wisconsin). (Mimeographed.)

3. Interview with Michael Parker, 26 August 1971.

4. Interview with Gail Paradise Kelly, 29 June 1971; also, interview with Michael Parker.

5. "Illinois Regional At-Large Elections," undated (Wisconsin State Historical Society SPU Collection). (Mimeographed.)

6. Ibid.

7. Interview with Maureen Kulbaitis Cassidy, 7-8 August 1971.

8. SPU, *Constitution*, adopted 29 April 1962 (SPU Papers, in the State Historical Society of Wisconsin). (Mimeographed.)

9. SPU, "Civil Rights," resolution adopted at the 1963 Annual Convention of the SPU (SPU Papers, in the State Historical Society of Wisconsin). (Mimeographed.)

10. "Cusick Reports," *SPU News Notes*, no. 7, 1964 (Wisconsin State Historical Society SPU Collection). (Mimeographed.)

11. "Vietnam," *SPU Bulletin*, November 1963 (SPU Papers, in the State Historical Society of Wisconsin).

12. Interview with Maureen Kulbaitis Cassidy, 7-8 August 1971.

13. Interview with Michael Parker, 26 August 1971.

14. Interview with David Kelly, 29 June 1971.

15. Interview with Gail Paradise Kelly, 29 June 1971.

16. Ibid.

17. Letter from Michael Parker to David McReynolds, 26 September 1961 (Tamiment Library YPSL Collection).

18. Letter from Michael Parker to Rachelle Horowitz, 19 November 1961 (Tamiment Library YPSL Collection).

19. Letter to Michael Parker, 12 May 1961 (SPU Papers, in the State Historical Society of Wisconsin).

20. See, for example, New York City (Off Campus Chapter), "Toward a Mass and Democratic Student Peace Union." Resolution to the 1963 SPU Convention (SPU Papers, in the State Historical Society of Wisconsin). (Mimeographed.)

21. Interview with Gail Paradise Kelly, 29 June 1971.

22. Daniel Rosenshine, "Resolution on Vietnam," Resolution submitted to the 1963 SPU Convention (SPU Papers, in the State Historical Society of Wisconsin). (Mimeographed.) Rosenshine was a member of the YSA, and in the late sixties became a leader of antiwar activities by the Socialist Workers party.

23. Letter from David McReynolds to Michael Parker, 21 September 1961 (SPU Papers, in the State Historical Society of Wisconsin).

24. Letter from Michael Parker to David McReynolds, 26 September 1961 (Tamiment Library YPSL Collection).

25. Philip Altbach, "The Student Movement—Dream and Reality," 15 November 1961 (SPU Papers, in the State Historical Society of Wisconsin). (Mimeographed.)

26. See, for example, letter from Al Haber to Michael Parker, 21 June 1961 (SPU Papers, in the State Historical Society of Wisconsin).

27. Interview with Michael Parker, 26 August 1971.

28. Interview with Gail Paradise Kelly, 29 June 1971.

29. Interview with David Kelly, 29 June 1971.

Chapter 4
On Theory

1. For a partisan history of the L.I.D. from 1905 to 1955, see Mina Weisenberg, *The L.I.D. Fifty Years of Democracy Education 1905-1955,* League for Industrial Democracy (New York: Tamiment Library L.I.D. Collection, 1955). For an account of the Student League for Industrial Democracy during the same period, see Harold Lewack, *Campus Rebels, S.L.I.D.* (New York: Tamiment Library SLID Collection, 1956).

2. Massimo Teodori, *The New Left: A Documentary History* (New York: Bobbs-Merrill, 1969).

3. Kirkpatrick Sale, *SDS* (New York: Random House, 1973).

4. National Executive Committee, SLID, "Statement on the World Situation," January 1951 (Tamiment Library SLID Collection). (Mimeographed.)

5. Letter to Susan Gyarmati, 10 March 1957 (Tamiment Library SLID Collection).

6. Letter from SLID Field Secretary, 9 April 1957 (Tamiment Library SLID Collection).

7. S.L.I.D., "Resolutions Approved by the 1957 National Convention," 6-7 September 1957 (Tamiment Library SLID Collection). (Mimeographed.)

8. Ibid, p. 1.

9. Ibid, p. 2.

10. Andre Schiffrin, "The Student Movement in the 1950's: A Reminiscence," in *Radical America,* 2, no. 3, (May-June 1968).

11. These figures are taken from registration records available in the Tamiment Library SLID Collection.

12. Letter from Al Haber to Charles Van Tassell, 31 July 1958 (Tamiment Library SLID Collection).

13. These were in April 1959; and Winter 1959-60 (Tamiment Library *Venture* Collection).

14. See, in particular, Robert Allan Haber, "From Protest to Radicalism," *Venture,* September 1960 (Tamiment Library *Venture* Collection).

15. "SDS 1960 Conference on Human Rights in the North Recommendations," *Venture,* September 1960 (Tamiment Library *Venture* Collection).

16. Ibid.

17. See "Student Radicalism—1960," article in the *SDS Voice,* July 1960 (Tamiment Library SDS Collection). The *SDS Voice* was an internal organ of SDS.

18. Ibid.

19. Robert A. Haber, "Progress Report and Organization Perspectives," 25 October 1960 (Tamiment Library SDS Collection). (Mimeographed.) The five functioning chapters were: University of Michigan, Yale, Syracuse, N.Y. City, Brooklyn College, and Western Reserve; those in active formation were: University of Chicago, Ohio Wesleyan, Villanova, Harvard, and University of Wisconsin.

20. L.I.D., "Minutes-Student Activities Committee," 12 December 1960 (Tamiment Library SDS Collection). (Mimeographed.)

21. Ibid.

22. S.D.S. "Minutes of NEC Meeting," 12 January 1961 (Tamiment Library SDS Collection). (Mimeographed.) Bob Ross was the member who supported Haber.

23. See Al Haber, "Memorandum on the Students for a Democratic Society," 20 May 1961 (Tamiment Library SDS Collection). (Mimeographed.)

24. Ibid. This inability to find volunteer help was a reflection of the fact that New York City members were associated with the opposition to Haber.

25. Letter from Al Haber to LID Board of Directors, 23 March 1961 (Tamiment Library SDS Collection).

26. Letter from Al Haber to Nathaniel Minkoff, 26 March 1961 (Tamiment Library SDS Collection).

27. Al Haber, "Proposal for the Continuity of the Student Department," 4 May 1961 (Tamiment Library SDS Collection). (Mimeographed.)

28. Letter from Al Haber to Isiah Minkoff, undated (Tamiment Library SDS Collection). Besides Haber, the other students were: Tom Hayden, Sandra Cason, Allan and Judy Guskin, Bob Walters, Paul Potter, and Mark Furstenberg.

29. Al Haber, "Memorandum on the Students for a Democratic Society," (Tamiment Library SDS Collection). (Mimeographed).

30. L.I.D., "Recommendations Presented to the L.I.D. Board of Directors," 24 May 1961 (Tamiment Library SDS Collection).

31. Al Haber, "Memo to LID-WDL," 13 September 1951 (Tamiment Library SDS Collection). (Mimeographed.)

32. See SDS, "Convention Bulletin Number One," 25 April 1962 (Tamiment Library SDS Collection). (Mimeographed.)

33. For a summary of activities, see ibid.

34. Cited in SDS National Executive Committee, "Relationship between SDS and LID." 12 July 1962 (Tamiment Library SDS Collection),p. 4. (Mimeographed.)

35. SDS, "Registration List—SDS Convention," 11-12 June 1962 (Tamiment Library SDS Collection). (Mimeographed.)

36. Cited in SDS-NEC, "Relationship Between SDS and LID."

37. Interview with Richard Flacks, 24 August 1971.

38. Ibid.

39. SDS, *Port Huron Statement,* June 1962 (Tamiment Library SDS Collection). (Mimeographed.)

40. Ibid., p. 1.

41. Ibid., p. 2.

42. Ibid., pp. 4-5.

43. Ibid., p. 5.

44. Ibid., p. 17.

45. Ibid., p. 25.

46. Ibid., pp. 51-52.

47. SDS, "Report on SDS Convention," 29 June 1962 (Tamiment Library SDS Collection). (Mimeographed.)

48. See C. Clark Kissinger, "The Birth of a Movement: SDS from 1960 to 1965," (SDS Papers, in the State Historical Society of Wisconsin). (Mimeographed.)

49. LID, "Minutes—Student Activities Committee Meeting," 28 June 1962 (Tamiment Library LID Collection). (Mimeographed.)

50. SDS-NEC, "Relationship Between SDS and LID," p. 7. This document describes the entire chronology of events surrounding the suspension and represented the formal appeal by the student group of the suspension.

51. Ibid., p. 8.

52. See "League for Industrial Democracy Statement of Principles: With Emphasis on the Relationship Between the LID and the SDS,"

August 1962, signed by Haber, Hayden, and the LID leaders (Tamiment Library LID Collection). (Mimeographed.)

53. LID, "Minutes—Student Activities Committee Meeting."

54. See, Irving Louis Horowitz, *Radicalism and the Revolt Against Reason* (Carbondale: Southern Illinois University, 1968).

55. SDS, *America and the New Era,* 1963 (SDS Papers, in the State Historical Society of Wisconsin) (Mimeographed.)

56. SDS, "Convention Report," undated in 1963 (SDS Papers, in the State Historical Society of Wisconsin.) (Mimeographed.) The quote is from the draft document before it was revised by the convention.

57. The draft document was titled *American Scene* and was prepared by Richard Flacks and Tom Hayden. See ibid.

58. SDS, *America and the New Era,* p. 20.

59. SDS, "National Council Minutes," 30 August-1 September 1963 (SDS Papers, in the State Historical Society of Wisconsin). (Mimeographed.)

60. Letter from Tom Hayden to Todd Gitlin, 2 August 1963 (SDS Papers, in the State Historical Society of Wisconsin).

61. SDS, "National Council Minutes," 1 September 1963.

62. SDS, "National Council Minutes," December 1963 (SDS Papers, in the State Historical Society of Wisconsin). (Mimeographed.)

63. Ibid. See also "Hayden Priority Proposal," (SDS Papers, in the State Historical Society of Wisconsin). (Mimeographed.) The final vote was twenty for the Hayden proposal and six for the Haber version.

64. Interview with Richard Flacks, 24 August 1971.

65. Interview with an SDS leader who wishes to remain anonymous.

66. Ad Hoc Committee for United States Action in the Crisis, "To JFK and Mr. K—STOP THIS GAME OF CHICKEN!" (SDS Papers in the State Historical Society of Wisconsin). (Mimeographed.) The "ad hoc committee" was an SDS operation.

67. Carl Oglesby, "Trapped in a System," speech at the March on Washington, 27 November 1965. Mimeographed pamphlet published by the Radical Education Project (Ann Arbor: 1970).

68. Articles in the February and March 1964 *SDS Bulletin* provide some detail on the issues involved. Particularly the articles by Todd Gitlin and Steve Max (SDS Papers, in the State Historical Society of Wisconsin).

69. Steve Max, "Words Butter No Parsnips: Remarks on the Nature of Community Political Organizing," *SDS Bulletin,* March 1964 (SDS Papers, in the State Historical Society of Wisconsin). (Mimeographed.)

70. Interview with Richard Flacks, 24 August 1971.

71. For an interesting discussion of this, see Gilbert Green, *The New Radicalism: Anarchist or Marxist* (New York: International Publishers, 1971). See also Irving Louis Horowitz.

72. Kirkpatrick Sale discussed this at some length, and it is supported by my own interviews with ERAP participants.

Chapter 5
On Practice

1. Interview with Susan Gyarmati, 23 May, 1971. See also Andre Schiffrin, "The Student Movement in the 1950s: A Reminiscence," in *Radical America* 2, no. 3 (May-June 1968).

2. I base this on the places that SLID was able to maintain chapters during the fifties. Susan Gyarmati was helpful providing information on the careers of some SLID members, although a few have been publicly visible. Eldon Clingan, for example, was for a time a member of the City Council in New York City.

3. See, for example, SDS-NEC, "Relationship Between SDS and LID," 12 July, 1962 (Tamiment Library SDS Collection). (Mimeographed.)

4. Ibid. Also, interview with Richard Flacks, 24 August 1971.

5. Al Haber, "Memorandum on the Students for a Democratic Society," 20 May, 1961 (Tamiment Library SDS Collection), p. 18. (Mimeographed.)

6. Al Haber, "Memorandum on the National Student Association Congress," 8 June, 1961 (Tamiment Library SDS Collection). (Mimeographed.)

7. Undated letter in file. (SDS Papers, in the State Historical Society of Wisconsin).

8. Tom Hayden, "Race and Politics Conference," undated memo (Tamiment Library SDS Collection). Also, see SDS-NEC, "Minutes —Meeting of the SDS-NEC Chapel Hill, May 6-7, 1962" (Tamiment Library SDS Collection). (Mimeographed.)

9. See, for example, C.Clark Kissinger, "The Birth of a Movement: SDS from 1960 to 1965" (SDS Papers, in the State Historical Society of Wisconsin). (Mimeographed.)

10. Interview with an SDS leader who wishes to remain anonymous.

11. Interview with Tom Hayden, 23 August 1971.

12. Ibid.

13. Ibid.

14. Ibid.

15. No systematic data on the family backgrounds of early SDS members is available, and I have relied on information supplied during personal interviews for this brief sketch. Kirkpatrick Sale, however, independently reports the same information. See Kirkpatrick Sale, *SDS* (New York: Random House, 1963), p. 89.

16. The series of reports Hayden wrote on his southern travels, for example, reflect this emphasis. These were later compiled and circulated as *Report from Mississippi* (SDS Papers, in the State Historical Society of Wisconsin). (Mimeographed.) I do not mean to suggest, however, that the students did not support the specific goals of the civil-rights campaigns —they did.

17. The writings of C. Wright Mills fostered an identification between "radicalism" and "Reason and Humanism," and his writings were widely read in SDS circles. Hayden, for example, had written a thesis on Mills at Michigan, and Mills's "Letter to the New Left," which first appeared in *New Left Review* (September-October 1960) was must reading for the young activists.

18. Interview with Paul Booth, 24 November 1971.

19. All those I interviewed indicated that this was the case, and Sale makes similar observations.

20. During those years the largest chapters were at the University of Michigan, Swarthmore, N.Y. City At-Large, and Harvard. The University of Chicago also had a large chapter. See organizational records in the SDS Papers, in the State Historical Society of Wisconsin.

21. See Richard Rothstein, "Representative Democracy in SDS," in *Liberation* 16, no. 9 (February 1972). He gives a very detailed analysis of this process.

22. Ibid.

23. Ibid. The new constitution created a "troika" of a national secretary, interorganizational secretary, and internal education secretary.

24. See, for example, SDS, "1964 National Convention Minutes," SDS National Council Meeting, 6 June 1964, and "Minutes of the SDS National Council Meeting, September 5-7, 1964," (SDS Papers, in the State Historical Society of Wisconsin). (Mimeographed.)

25. Ibid. Also see Richard Rothstein.

26. Carl Wittman and Thomas Hayden, "An Interracial Movement of the Poor?" in *The New Student Left,* eds. Mitchell Cohen and Dennis Hale (Boston: Beacon Press, 1966), p. 210. The original article was written for a meeting of the SDS National Council in the winter of 1963.

27. At the ERAP National Committee Meeting of 7 and 8 November 1964, for example, Rennie Davis, Paul Potter, Todd Gitlin, Richard Rothstein, and others discussed "SDS Expansion," including the question of adult organizing, campus vs. community work, etc. See *ERAP Newsletter,* 16-23 November 1964 (SDS Papers, in the State Historical Society of Wisconsin). (Mimeographed.)

28. Dick Flacks made some similar observations in an open letter, 25 January 1965, which was circulated to NC members (SDS Papers, in the State Historical Society of Wisconsin).

29. For a sympathetic analysis of the early development of ERAP projects, see Andrew Kopkind, "Of, By and For the Poor—The New Generation of Student Organizers," in *The New Republic,* 19 June 1965.

30. Cited in "1963 National Convention—National Secretary Report," (SDS Papers, in the State Historical Society of Wisconsin). (Mimeographed.)

31. Cited in C.Clark Kissinger, "The Birth of a Movement: SDS from 1960 to 1965," (SDS Papers, in the State Historical Society of Wisconsin). (Mimeographed.)

32. Ibid.

33. Clark Kerr, *The Uses of the University* (Cambridge: Harvard University Press, 1963).

34. Mario Savio, "An End to History." An edited version of the speech appeared in *Humanity,* December 1964.

35. For a collection of documents and interpretations of the FSM, see Seymour Martin Lipset & Sheldon S. Wolin, eds. *The Berkeley Student Revolt* (New York: Doubleday, 1965). For an account sympathetic to the FSM, see Hal Draper, *Berkeley: The New Student Revolt* (New York: Grove Press, 1965).

36. PREP, "New Crisis in Vietnam," 29 February 1964 (SDS Papers, in the State Historical Society of Wisconsin). (Mimeographed.)

37. See, for example, Kirkpatrick Sale, p. 171.

38. SDS, "A Call to All Students to March on Washington to End the War in Vietnam," undated (SDS Papers, in the State Historical Society of Wisconsin). (Mimeographed.)

39. Martin Roysher & Charles Capper, "The March as a Political Tactic," (SDS Papers, in the State Historical Society of Wisconsin). (Mimeographed.)

40. Ibid.

41. C. Clark Kissinger.

42. SDS, *Port Huron Statement,* June 1962 (SDS Papers, in the State Historical Society of Wisconsin). p. 7. (Mimeographed.)

43. C. Wright Mills, "Letter to the New Left," in *The New Radicals,* eds. Paul Jacobs and Saul Landau (New York: Vintage Books, 1966), p. 111. The article originally appeared in *New Left Review,* September-October 1960.

44. SDS, *America and the New Era,* June 1963 (SDS Papers, in the State Historical Society of Wisconsin). p. 24. (Mimeographed.)

45. No comprehensive account of the ERAP experience has yet been written, and the documents available provide little insight into the actual organizing experience. One partial account which is helpful is Todd Gitlin & Nancy Hollander, *Uptown* (New York: Harper & Row, 1970). I have relied on information supplied during personal interviews, and Marilyn Katz was especially helpful in recounting her experience in JOIN.

46. FSM, "We Want a University," Fall 1964 (SDS Papers, in the State Historical Society of Wisconsin). (Mimeographed.)

Chapter 6
The New Left and American Society

1. Quoted in the FSM document, *We Want A University* (SDS Papers, in the State Historical Society of Wisconsin), p. 9. (Mimeographed.)

2. For an excellent review of these arguments, see Donald Hodges, "Old and New Working Classes," in *Radical America* 5, no. 1 (January-February 1971), pp. 11-32. Also see Bettina Aptheker, *The Academic Rebellion in the United States* (Secaucus, N.J.: Citadel Press, 1972).

3. One of the earliest examples of new working class theories is Serge Mallet, *La Nouvelle Classe Ouvriere* (Paris: Seuil, 1963).

4. Ernest Mandel, "Where is America Going?" reprinted in *Leviathan* 1, no. 5 (September 1969), p. 23.

5. Richard Flacks, "Strategies for Radical Social Change," in *Social Policy* 1, no. 6 (March-April 1971), p. 10.

6. Ibid.

7. See, for example, Abbott L. Ferriss, *Indicators of Trends in American Education* (New York: Russell Sage Foundation, 1969), p. 21.

8. Ibid., pp. 52-53.

9. Ibid., pp. 185-99.

10. Ibid.

11. For a much more detailed discussion of this change, see Fritz Machlup, *The Production and Distribution of Knowledge in the United States* (Princeton, N.J.: Princeton University Press, 1962); also see, Bettina Aptheker.

12. See, for example, Bettina Aptheker, chapter 5.

13. George S. Odiorne and Arthur S. Hann, *Effective College Recruiting* (Ann Arbor: University of Michigan, Bureau of Industrial Relations, 1961), p. 176.

14. Kenneth J. Neubeck, *Corporate Response to Urban Crisis* (Lexington, Mass.: D.C. Heath & Co., 1974).

15. See, for example, Richard Flacks, *Youth and Social Change* (Chicago: Markham, 1971).

16. While there is no comprehensive time-series data on this pattern, several case studies strongly illustrate the trend. For a study of the California Master Plan, see Bettina Aptheker.

17. James P. O'Brien, *The Development of a New Left in the United States, 1960-1965*, unpublished Ph.D. dissertation (Dept. of History, University of Wisconsin, 1971).

18. See, for example, Richard Flacks, "Who Protests? The Social Bases of the Student Movement," in *Protest! Student Activism in America,* eds. Julian Foster and Durward Long (New York: William Morrow & Co., 1970), pp. 134-57.

19. Richard Flacks, *Youth and Social Change* (Chicago: Markham Publishing Co., 1971).

20. See, for example, W. Lloyd Warner, *The Social Life of a Modern Community*, vol. 1. "Yankee City Series" (New Haven: Yale University Press, 1941); also see R. S. Lynd and H. M. Lynd, *Middletown* (New York: Harcourt, Brace & Co., 1929).

21. William H. Whyte, *The Organization Man* (Garden City, N.Y.: Doubleday, 1956), p. 297.

22. Ibid.

23. See, for example, Abbott L. Ferriss, *Indicators of Change in the American Family* (New York: Russell Sage Foundation, 1970).

24. See, for example, Urie Bronfenbrenner, "Socialization & Social Class Through Time and Space," in *Readings in Social Psychology,* eds. E. E. Maccoby, T. M. Newcomb, E. C. Hartley (New York: Holt, Rinehart & Winston, 1958).

25. Ibid.

26. Melvin Kohn, *Class and Conformity: A Study in Values* (Homewood, Ill.: Dorsey Press, 1969).

27. Ibid., p. 111.

28. Ibid., p. 142.

29. Melvin L. Kohn and Carmi Schooler, "Occupational Experience and Psychological Functioning: An Assessment of Reciprocal Effects," in *American Sociological Review* 38, no. 1 (February 1973).

30. Melvin Kohn.

31. Carmi Schooler, "Social Antecedents of Adult Psychological Functioning," in *American Journal of Sociology,* September 1972.

32. See, for example, Richard Flacks, *Youth and Social Change* (Chicago: Markham, 1971); also see Kenneth Keniston, *Young Radicals* (New York: Harcourt, Brace & World, 1968).

33. David Riesman, with Nathan Glazer and Reuel Denney, *The Lonely Crowd* (New Haven: Yale University Press, 1960).

34. Based on GNP figures in constant dollars. See U.S. Department of Labor, *Manpower Report of the President, 1972* (Washington: U.S. Government Printing Office, 1972), table G-2, p. 325.

35. Ibid., table C-1, p. 265.

36. James O'Connor, "Some Contradictions of Advanced U.S. Capitalism," in *Social Theory and Practice,* Spring 1970. See also Fritz Machlup and Bettina Aptheker.

37. Cited in Donald Clark Hodges, "Old and New Working Classes," in *Radical America* 5, no. 1. (January-February 1971).

38. A. A. Berle, *Power Without Property* (New York: Harcourt, Brace & World, 1959), p. 18.

39. Ferdinand Lundberg, *The Rich and the Super-Rich* (New York: Lyle Stuart, 1968), p. 296.

40. Ibid.

41. *Statistical Abstract of the United States,* table 347, p. 222.

42. Ibid.

43. This is precisely the distinction made by C. Wright Mills in *White Collar* (London: Oxford University Press, 1951).

44. Donald Clark Hodges.

45. I have not attempted such a resolution here. I have only tried to indicate the complexities that flow from a consideration of two of the issues involved. The literature on new working class theories continues to grow, but there is not yet any sign of an emerging consensus of the definitional problems—let alone, on an interpretation of findings.

46. For a more detailed discussion of this aspect, see Martin Oppenheimer, "What is the New Working Class?" in *New Politics* 10, (Fall 1972).

Chapter 7
Conclusion: The Beginning of the Decline

1. Carl Oglesby, "Notes on a Decade Ready for the Dustbin," in *Liberation,* August-September 1969.

2. Greg Calvert, "In White America: Radical Consciousness and Social Change," in the *National Guardian,* 25 March 1967.

3. For a view of PL's relation to SDS sympathetic to PL, see Alan Adelson, *SDS: A Profile* (New York: Scribners, 1971); for an opposite view, see Kirkpatrick Sale, *SDS* (New York: Random House, 1973).

4. See, for example, "You Don't Need a Weatherman to Tell Which Way the Wind Blows," reprinted in Harold Jacobs, *Weatherman,* (California: Ramparts Press, 1970).

5. For a more detailed discussion, see Kirkpatrick Sale.

6. Members of the New York staff, "Look Out Cleveland," in *Leviathan* 1, no. 8. During 1969 and 1970, *Leviathan* was the main theoretical journal of the New Left, but the same ideological splits that fragmented the movement led to its dissolution in late 1970.

7. See, for example, Milton Mankoff and Richard Flacks, "The Changing Social Base of the American Student Movement," in *The New Pilgrims,* eds. Philip G. Altbach & Robert S. Laufer (New York: David McKay, 1972).

8. Donald Clark Hodges, "Old and New Working Classes," in *Radical America* 5, no. 1 (January-February 1971).

9. Tamar Pitch, "Radical Sociology and New Working Class Theories," unpublished paper (Department of Sociology, University of Connecticut, 1973).

Index

Index

A & T College, Greensboro, N.C., 21
ADA. *See* Americans for Democratic Action
Adams, Rebecca, 73, 90, 92
AFL. *See* American Federation of Labor
Albany, Ga., 24
Algerian revolution, 47
Altbach, Philip, xi
America and the New Era (1963 SDS statement), 80-86, 103
American Federation of Labor (AFL), 33-35
    merger with CIO, 34-35
American Friends Service Committee, 39, 51, 59
Americans for Democratic Action (ADA), 36-37, 90
Ann Arbor, Mich., 96
Antioch College, 48
Aptheker, Bettina, 109
Atlanta, Ga., 92

"Back to Africa" campaign (Garvey), 19
Barry, Marion, 23
Beat movement, 47-48
Berkeley, Calif., 27, 52
Berle, Adolph, 121
Bevel, James 22
Birmingham, Ala., 24, 25
Black movement, 132
    civil rights movement, 19-25
Black Muslims, 19
Black Panthers, 128, 132
Bolshevik Revolution, 36
Booth, Paul, 73, 77, 85, 90, 92, 95, 104
Boston, Mass., 89
Bronfenbrenner, Urie, 116, 117
Brooklyn College, 71
Burlage, Robb, 92
Bus boycott, Montgomery, Ala., 20

California, University of (Berkeley), 48, 98-99
    SLATE, 27, 57, 91
California, University of (Riverside)
    DECLARE, 27
Calkins, Ken, 51, 52
Calvert, Greg, 129
Campus Americans for Democratic Action, 89
Capitalism, 108, 115, 119, 133
    knowledge as tool of production, 120, 123-125; occupational structure, 121-123; postwar economic growth, 120-123

Central Intelligence Agency (CIA), 39, 46, 47, 68
Chabot, Joe, 82
Chapel Hill, N.C., 54
Chicago, Ill., 52, 53, 82
Chicago, University of, 48, 53, 71, 90
    POLIT, 27, 90
Child rearing policies, 116-119
CIA. *See* Central Intelligence Agency
CIO. *See* Congress of Industrial Organizations
City University of New York, 48
Civil rights movement, 108
    growth of movement, 19-25; nonviolence ideology, 21-25; SDS and, 73, 93-94
Class structure
    effect of changing capitalism on, 121-123; New Left and, 120-123; and postwar growth economy, 120-123. *See also* Society
CNVA. *See* Committee for Nonviolent Action
Cold war, 27, 54, 76, 80
Collectives, 131
Columbia University, 71
Committee for Nonviolent Action (CNVA), 28, 40, 51, 53
Committee on Political Education (AFL-CIO), 35
Communes, 131
Communism
    Port Huron Statement on, 76; repression of, in U.S., 36-39; SPU and, 56; trade union movement and, 33-35; Twentieth Party Congress, 37, 43. *See also* Labor Youth League
Congress of Cultural Freedom, 39
Congress of Industrial Organizations (CIO), 33-35; merger with AFL, 34-35
Congress of Racial Equality (CORE), 20, 21, 23, 27, 66, 69, 73, 90
    sit-in campaigns, 21
CORE. *See* Congress of Racial Equality
Cornell University, 48
Cuba, 54
    Bay of Pigs invasion, 83; missile crisis, 83, 84
Culture, cultural nationalism
    political vs. cultural opposition, 131-132, 133-136

Davis, Rennie, 65, 90, 92, 96
Debs, Eugene V., 38

DECLARE, 27
Democracy
New Left and, 80; participatory democracy (*Port Huron Statement*), 63, 75-76
Dentzler, William T., 47
Depression (1930s), 35
Detroit, Mich., 17
Dixiecrats, 44
Dodd, Sen. Thomas, 28

Economic Research and Action Project, SDS (ERAP), 81, 82, 85, 86, 87, 96, 97, 99, 100, 103, 128, 131
Education
financing of, 112-113; influences of, on New Left development, 111-114; knowledge as tool of production, 120, 123-125; rising enrollment, 111-112; role and function of university, 136-137; school desegregation, 19; structural systematic changes, 112-114; and student values, 114; technology and, 113
ERAP. *See* Economic Research and Action Project, SDS

Family structure, 115-119
Fanon, Frantz, 22
Farmer, James, 66
FDR Four Freedoms Club (New York), 73
Fellowship of Reconciliation (FOR), 22, 39, 40, 51
Ferlingetti, Lawrence, 48
Feuer, Lewis, 8, 108
on student movements, 4-6
Flacks, Richard, ix, 4, 6, 7, 8, 9, 85, 91, 92, 104, 109, 110, 111, 114, 115, 119, 123
FOR. *See* Fellowship of Reconciliation
Free Speech Movement, Berkeley (FSM), 98-99, 104, 108
Freedom Rides, 23
FSM. *See* Free Speech Movement, Berkeley

Garman, Betty, 92
Garvey, Marcus, 19
Ginsberg, Allan, 48
Gitlin, Todd, 90, 92, 95
Goodman, Paul, 107
Greensboro, N.C., 21

Haber, Robert Allan (Al), 68, 78, 81, 89, 90, 91
heads SLID-SDS, 69-73
Harrington, Michael, 42, 43
Harvard University, 67, 71, 90, 92

Hayden, Sandra Cason, 73, 90, 95
Hayden, Tom, 65, 72, 73, 78, 79, 82, 83, 85, 90, 91, 92, 93
Hitler-Stalin Pact, 36
Hodges, Donald, 122
Horowitz, Irving L., 80
Housing
"restrictive covenant" legislation, 19
Humphrey, Hubert, 84
Hungary, invasion of, 43

Illinois, University of
SCOPE, 27
Independent Socialist League (ISL), xi, 38, 42, 43
International Union of Students (IUS), 46
ISL. *See* Independent Socialist League
IUS. *See* International Union of Students

Jeffrey, Sharon, 92
Jenkins, Tim, 24, 73, 90
Jones, Charles, 24

Kaunda, Kenneth, 40
Keniston, Kenneth, ix, 9, 109, 119
Kennedy administration, 24, 83
Kennedy, John, 83
Kerouac, Jack, 48
Kerr, Clark, 98
Khrushchev, Nikita, 43
King, Martin Luther, Jr., 20
Kissinger, C. Clark, 78, 90, 104
Knowledge
as tool of production, 120, 123-125
Kohn, Melvin, xii, 117, 118
Kolko, Gabriel, 66
Korean War, 34, 41, 46

Labor. *See* Trade union movement
Labor force
composition of, 32-33
Labor Youth League (LYL), xi, 41, 91
"Statement of Principles," 41
Lafayette, Bernard, 22-23
Laos situation, 52
Lasch, Christopher, 39
Lawson, Rev. James, 22, 23
League for Industrial Democracy (LID), xi, 21, 39, 65, 66, 70, 78, 79, 89, 93, 100
SDS and, 71-73
Left, American
pacifism and, 39-40; post World War II situation, 35-49; young American left (1950s), 40-49. *See also* New Left; Old Left
Lewis, John, 23
Lewis, John L., 34

163

Liberalism
New Left and, 83-86
Liberation magazine, 40
Liberation News Service, 133
LID. *See* League for Industrial Democracy
Lundberg, Ferdinand, 121
LYL. *See* Labor Youth League
Lynd, R.S. and H.M., 116

Malcolm X, 20
Mandel, Ernest, 110
Marches on Washington (1963, 1965), 25, 99, 100
Marshall Plan, 34
Marx, Karl, 9
Marxism, 129
New Left and, 109-110, 130; "orthodox," vs. "critical" theory, x
Max, Steve, 77, 78, 85, 92
M'boya, Tom, 40
McCarthy Era, 31, 40, 66
McKinnie, Lester, 23
McNamara, Robert, 83
McReynolds, David, 52, 57, 59
Meany, George, 34, 35
MFDP. *See* Mississippi Freedom Democratic party
Michigan, University of, 48, 68, 69, 71, 83, 91, 113
VOICE, 27, 90
Michigan Daily, 72, 90, 91
Miles, Michael
on student manipulation, 2
Mills, C. Wright, 9, 102
"white collar" occupations study, 32
Mississippi Freedom Democratic party (MFDP), 83, 84, 97, 128
Mississippi Summer Project, 97, 131
Monsonis, James, 73, 77
Montgomery, Ala., 24
bus boycott, 20
Moscow, U.S.S.R., 28
Moses, Bob, 24
Murray, Philip, 34
Muste, A.J., 40

NAACP. *See* National Association for the Advancement of Colored People
Nash, Diane, 22, 24
Nashville, Tenn., 21, 22, 23
National Association for the Advancement of Colored People (NAACP), 19, 20, 21, 27
National Committee for a SANE Nuclear Policy, 28, 100
National Coordinating Committee Against the War in Vietnam, 128

National Council, SDS (NC), 95, 96, 97, 99, 101
National Executive Committee, SLID (NEC), 66, 68, 72, 77, 78, 95
National Mobilization Committee Against the War (Vietnam), 128
National Peace Action Coalition, 129
National Student Association (NSA), 24, 27, 46-47, 73, 74, 83, 89, 90, 91
National Student Christian Federation, 74
National Urban League, 19
NC. *See* National Council, SDS
NEC. *See* National Executive Committee, SLID
Neubeck, Kenneth, 113
New Deal, 19, 35, 36, 37
New Left, 6-8
American class structure and, 120-123; communes and collectives, 131; family background and, 4, 115-119; foundations for, 26-29; "generational conflict" and, 108-109; higher education and, 111-114; "intelligentsia" theory, 115; liberalism and, 83-86; as manipulation of students, 2; Marxism and, 109-110, 130; "new working class" theory and, 109-110; objective vs. subjective identity, 133-136; origins, 18-19, 114, 119, 123; as outcome of social and economic change, 123-125, 133; political character, 2-3; political vs. cultural opposition, 131-132, 133-136; *Port Huron Statement* on, 77; post-1966 development, 127-137; "post-scarcity" theory and, 109-110; post-sixties characteristics, 137; "psychological" explanations, 3-4; SDS and, 65, 69-88; SLID and, 65-69; as social force, 132-136; strategies for change, 107-125; value systems, 115-125. *See also* Left, American
The New Left Review, 18
New Mobilization Committee Against the War (Vietnam), 128
New York, N.Y., 28, 89, 96
New York City At-Large (SDS chapter), 71
New York Times, 27
Ngu, Madame, 54
Niagara Movement, 19
Nonviolence ideology
of civil rights movement, 21-25
North Carolina, University of, 90
Northwestern University, 48
NSA. *See* National Student Association

Nuclear weapons, tests, 27-28, 40
    partial test ban treaty, 52

Oberlin College, 48, 57, 73, 90, 92
O'Brien, James, ix, 6-8, 44, 114
O'Connor, James, 120
Oglesby, Carl, 84, 100, 129
Old Left, 129, 134-135
    vs. New Left, 28-29, 65; SDS and, 78-80;
        SPU and, 58-61. See also Left,
        American
Ollman, Bertell, 11

Pacifism
    American (1950s), 39-40; radical pacifists,
        (SPU), 53
Peace Corps, 83
Peace movement, 40
Peace Research and Education Project, SDS
    (PREP), 85, 96, 97, 99
Peace walks, 52, 53, 99
    San Francisco to Moscow Walk for Peace,
        28
People's Coalition for Peace and Justice, 129
PEP. See Political Education Project, SDS
PHS. See Port Huron Statement
PIC. See Political Issues Club
PL. See Progressive Labor party
POLIT, 27, 90
Political Education Project, SDS (PEP)
    (1964), 85, 97
Political Issues Club (PIC), 68, 91
Politics
    multi-issue vs. single-issue organizations,
        26-29; origins of political activity,
        18-19; political vs. cultural opposi-
        tion, 131-132, 133-136; post World
        War II, 31-49; of SPU, 52-54; stu-
        dent political parties, 27-29
Port Huron, Mich., 17, 78, 80, 85, 89, 91, 92,
    95, 97
Port Huron Statement, 17, 18, 63, 81, 85, 86,
    93, 95
    evaluated, 73-80
Potter, Paul, 90, 92
Prague, Czechoslovakia, 46
Praxis
    Marxist definition, x
PREP. See Peace Research and Education
    Project, SDS
Progressive Labor party (PL), 130, 135
Progressive Student League, Oberlin, 73, 90
Progressive Youth Organizing Committee
    (PYOC), 57, 74, 78
PYOC. See Progressive Youth Organizing
    Committee

Radical Education Project, SDS, 85
Raleigh, N.C., 23
Reuther, Walter, 34, 35
Revolutionary Youth Movement, 130, 135
Riesman, David, 119
Ross, Bob, 72, 78, 92
Rossman, Michael, 15
ROTC protest, 52
Rothstein, Richard, 92
Rustin, Bayard, 40
RYM. See Revolutionary Youth Movement

Sale Kirkpatrick, 65
San Francisco, Calif., 28
SANE. See National Committee for a SANE
    Nuclear Policy; Student Committee
    for a SANE Nuclear Policy
Schachtman, Max, 39, 43
Schlesinger, Arthur, Jr., 36
Schooler, Carmi, 118
Schools
    desegregation of, 19. See also Education
SCLC. See Southern Christian Leadership
    Conference
SCOPE, 27
SDS. See Students for a Democratic Society
Selma, Ala., 24, 25
Sit-in campaigns (1960), 21, 23, 52
SLATE. See Slate of Candidates
Slate of Candidates (SLATE), Berkeley, 57,
    91
    aims, 27
SLID. See Student League for Industrial
    Democracy
Smith, Kelly Miller, 22
SNCC. See Student Nonviolent Coordinat-
    ing Committee
Socialist Party (U.S.), 37-39, 43, 51
    merger with Independent Socialist
        League, 43
Socialist Workers party (SWP), xi, 38, 44
Society
    New Left as social force, 132-136. See also
        Class structure
Sociology
    American studies in, 9-10; Mills on, 9
Southern Christian Leadership Conference
    (SCLC), 21, 22, 23; formation of, 20
Soviet Union
    postwar U.S. relations, 36-39
Spring Mobilization Committee Against the
    War (Vietnam), 128
SPU. See Student Peace Union
Stalin, Josef, 18, 37, 43, 56
Student Committee for a SANE Nuclear Pol-
    icy, 28, 51, 56-57, 59

Student League for Industrial Democracy (SLID), xi, 26, 42; activism of, 69; anticommunism of, 66; background of leaders, 89; becomes SDS, 69; New Left and, 65-69; "Statement on the World Situation," 66. *See also* SDS
Student Mobilization Committee, 130
Student movements
Feuer on, 4-6
Student Nonviolent Coordinating Committee (SNCC), xi, 22, 23, 69, 72, 73, 74, 89, 90, 91, 94, 128, 132.
voter registration drives, 24-25
Student Peace Union (SPU), xi, 13, 65, 89, 90 anticommunism, 56; assessment of, 58-61; Old Left and, 58-61; origins and development, 51-52; politics of, 52-54; Statement of Purpose (1959, 1962), 52, 54, 57, 58; and YPSL, 52-58, 59, 60
Students for a Democratic Society (SDS), xi, 13, 23, 39, 69, 134, 135
America and the New Era (1963 statement), 80-86, 103; anticommunism of, 72, 73; background of leaders, 89-94, 115, 136; civil rights movement, 73, 93-94; ERAP, 81, 82, 85, 86, 87, 96, 97, 99, 100, 103, 128, 131; FSM, (Berkeley), 98-99, 104, 108; Human Rights in the North Conference (1960), 69-70, 90; identity search, 101-104; Ideologies, Politics, and Controversies of the Student Movement Conference (1961), 72-73; indictment of leaders (1970), 17; LID and, 71-73; New Left and, 17-19, 65, 69-88; (*see also* New Left); Old Left and, 78-80; organizational structure, 94-97; Peace Research and Education Project, 85, 96, 97, 99; Political Education Project (1964), 85, 97; Port Huron, Mich., meeting (1962), 17, 73-83, 85, 86, 93, 95; protest and resistance techniques, 128-131; Radical Education Project, 85; role of women in, 131-132; "Student Radicalism-1960" (annual convention), 70; university role and, 111. *See also* SLID
Suicidalism
in student movements, 4
Supreme Court (U.S.)
housing desegregation, 19; school desegregation, 19, 20
Swarthmore College, 73, 90, 92

SWP. *See* Socialist Workers party
Syracuse University, 71

Taft, Philip, 34
Taft-Hartley Act, 33, 34
Tallahassee, Fla., 21
Teodori, Massimo, 65
Terrorism
in student movements, 4
Theory, "critical" vs. "orthodox" Marxism, x
Thomas, Norman, 37
Thompson, E.P.
The Making of the English Working Class, x, 105
Trade union movement, 36, 108
post World War II consolidation, 32-35
Trotsky, Leon, 38
Troy, Leo, 32
Turn Toward Peace, 82

UAW. *See* United Automobile Workers
Underground Press Syndicate, 133
United Automobile Workers (UAW), 34, 35, 81
United Labor Policy Committee, 34
United Mineworkers, 34
United Steelworkers, 34

Value systems
conformist vs. self-directed, 118-119; influence of, on New Left, 115-125; occupations and, 117-118; self-direction and, 117-119; social class and, 117
Venture, 31, 69, 71
-Vietnam War protest, 44, 54, 83, 84, 85, 99, 128
Vivian, C.T., 22
VOICE, 27, 68, 90
Voter registration drives, 24-25

Wallace, Henry, 34
War Resistors League, 39, 52
Warner, Lloyd, 116
Weathermen, 130-131
Webb, Lee, 92
Wedding within the War, The, 15. See also Rossman, Michael
Western Reserve College, 71
Whyte, William H., 116
Wisconsin Liberal Club, 26
Wisconsin, University of, 46, 89
Women's movement, 132
Worker, 92
World Federation of Trade Unions, 34

World War II, 22, 31, 35, 36, 41, 112, 113, 116, 118, 120

Yale University, 71, 89
Yarmolinsky, Adam, 83
Young Christian Students, 74
Young Democrats, 27, 74
Young People's Socialist League (YPSL), xi, 27, 42, 43, 44, 70, 71, 89, 90
  SPU and, 52-58, 59, 60

Young Socialist Alliance (YSA), xi, 44, 57, 58, 90, 130
Young Socialist League (YSL), xi, 39, 42, 44
  socialist realignment and unity debate, 43
YPSL. *See* Young People's Socialist League
YSA. *See* Young Socialist Alliance
YSL. *See* Young Socialist League

Zellner, Bob, 73, 90

About the Author

George R. Vickers is thirty-one years old and was born in Evanston, Illinois. His undergraduate study at Kendall College and Northwestern University was periodically interrupted by full-time participation in the civil-rights and New Left movements. He obtained his Ph.D. in sociology from Washington University in St. Louis, taught at the University of Connecticut, and is currently a staff sociologist at the Russell Sage Foundation. In 1968 he edited *Dialogue on Violence* and is the author of several articles on the New Left.